Student's Book

CONTENTS

CONTENTS

Welcome!

Introducing yourself and others
Present simple: *be* and personal pronouns
Questions: *What …? Where …? Who …?*

1 READING

🔘 1.01 Read the dialogue. Who is from England?

2 AFTER READING

Complete the sentences.

1 Pierre is from _____.
2 _____ is from Russia.
3 Jake is the boy from _____.
4 _____ is from Spain.
5 The names of the girls are _____, _____ and _____.
6 _____ is a teacher.

Welcome!

NFI STUDENT EXCHANGE

| Home | About | StudentZone | Staff |

Students from **New Friends International** are with students in England for ten days.

International Students
1 Katya – Russia
2 Jake – the USA
3 Teresa – Spain
4 Pierre – Switzerland

Brighton High School
5 Adam
6 Emily

3 LISTENING

🔘 1.02 Listen and complete.

ADAM   Who's she?
EMILY   Her name is _____.
ADAM   Is she American?
EMILY   No, she isn't.
ADAM   Where's she from?
EMILY   She's from _____.

Who is she and where is she from?

4 SPEAKING

Look at the web page. Ask and answer questions about the exchange students.

Who's he/she?   His/Her name is _____.

Where's he/she from?   He's/She's from _____.

5 ROLE PLAY

You are a famous person. Introduce yourself to other famous people.

A Hi, my name is Miley. What's your name?
B Hello. I'm Brad and this is Robert.
C It's nice to meet you.

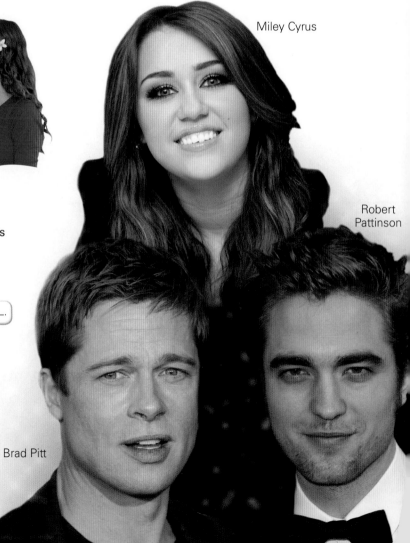

Miley Cyrus

Robert Pattinson

Brad Pitt

6 SPEAKING

Find the countries for these nationalities on page 8.

> American   English   Russian   Spanish   Swiss

Now ask and answer questions about the exchange students.

A What's his/her name?
B _____
A Is he/she (*nationality*)?
B Yes, he/she is. OR No, he/she isn't. He/She's (*nationality*).

7 PRONUNCIATION

🔘 1.03   Listen and repeat.

> /w/ we   welcome   what   where
> /h/ he   her   his   who

8 VOCABULARY

🔘 1.04   Listen and repeat.

Word Bank	Numbers		
0	oh/zero		
1	one	11	eleven
2	two	12	twelve
3	three	13	thirteen
4	four	14	fourteen
5	five	15	fifteen
6	six	16	sixteen
7	seven	17	seventeen
8	eight	18	eighteen
9	nine	19	nineteen
10	ten	20	twenty

9 GAME *BINGO*

Choose nine numbers from 1–20. Write them on the Bingo card.

🔘 1.05   Now listen and cross out (✗) the numbers you hear.

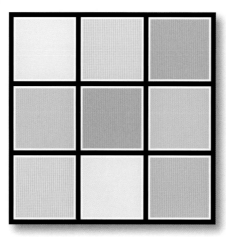

10 LISTENING

🔘 1.06   Listen to Mr Ward. Complete the information.

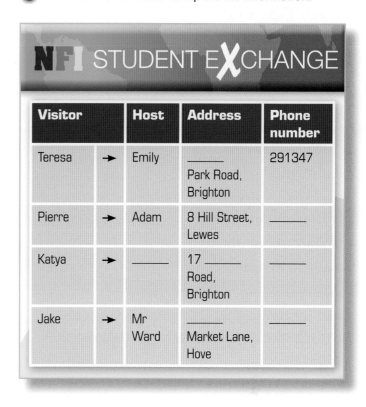

NFI STUDENT EXCHANGE

Visitor		Host	Address	Phone number
Teresa	→	Emily	_____ Park Road, Brighton	291347
Pierre	→	Adam	8 Hill Street, Lewes	_____
Katya	→	_____	17 _____ Road, Brighton	_____
Jake	→	Mr Ward	Market Lane, Hove	_____

11 WRITING

Write down the address and phone number of three students.

> What's your address?

> What's your phone number?

LANGUAGE WORKOUT

Complete.

Present simple: *be* and personal pronouns

Affirmative

Full forms	Contractions
I am	_____
you are	you're
he/she/it is	he's/she's/it's
we are	_____
they are	they're

Negative	Questions
I'm not	am I?
you aren't	_____?
he/she/it _____	is he/she/it?
we aren't	are we?
they _____	_____?

▶**Answers and Practice**
Language File page 114

PREVIEW

COMMUNICATIVE AIMS
LEARNING HOW TO ...

1 Talk about possessions
2 Tell the time
3 Describe places
4 Talk about your family
5 Describe people
6 Talk about ability
7 Give instructions

TOPICS AND VOCABULARY

Possessions

Numbers

Family

Prepositions of place

Months

Colours

Clothes

Music

Phone calls and messages

1 Match the pictures (A–F) with six items in the Topics and Vocabulary box.

2 Put the words into categories.

Clothes

Family

Music

brother piano jacket trousers sister daughter band drums skirt guitar grandfather mother rap T-shirt pullover

Can you play the saxophone?

A

My mother is on the right.

B

Look – it's on my ID card.

C

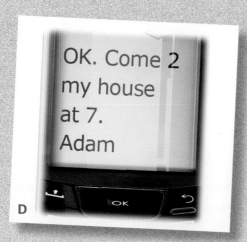

D

F

She has a long scarf round her neck.

E

Rosie Raven has green eyes and black hair.

5 Do the questionnaire with three other students. Tell another group the answers.

3 Match the words with the pictures.

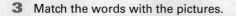

bag   cap   camera   jeans   phone   window

Favourites Questionnaire

What's your favourite …?

* Colour
* Number
* Month
* Musical instrument

4 🔘 1.07   Listen to extracts 1–3 from Units 1 and 2. Match them with these topics.

A A family
B A place
C A band

Believe it or not!

Four is the only number in English that has the same number of letters as its meaning.

1 That's a great bag!

Talking about possessions
this/that   Indefinite article

1 OPENER

Who is in the photo? Guess: What are they talking about?

2 READING

🔘 1.08   Read the dialogue. Which sentence matches the photo?

ADAM   Hi, Teresa! I'm Adam Campbell.
TERESA Sorry? Adam what?
ADAM   Campbell. C-A-M-P-B-E-double L.
TERESA Oh, I see. My surname is Navarro.
ADAM   How do you spell it?
TERESA N-A-V-A-R-R-O. Look – it's on my ID card.
ADAM   That's a great bag!
TERESA What? Oh yes! This is my favourite bag.
ADAM   What else is in it?
TERESA Guess!
ADAM   OK. A bottle of water?
TERESA Right!
ADAM   An MP3 player?
TERESA Yes.
ADAM   Um. A photograph of your boyfriend?
TERESA No! A photo of my family – it's in my ... What's this in English?
ADAM   It's called a wallet. Are *all* your things in that bag?
TERESA No! That's my rucksack over there. Now it's my turn! What's in your bag?

3 AFTER READING

Answer the questions about Teresa.

1 What's her surname?
2 What's in her bag?
3 What's in her wallet?

Your response What's in your bag?

4 PRONUNCIATION

🔘 1.09   Listen and repeat the alphabet.

A B C D E F G H I J K L M
N O P Q R S T U V W X Y Z

A H J K   B C D E G P T V   F L M N S X Z
I Y   O   Q U W   R

Now listen and write five words.

5 SPEAKING

Point at the people in the photo on pages 6–7. Ask and answer.

A What's his/her name?
B _____
A How do you spell it?
B _____

Extension Point at students in your class, and ask and answer the same questions.

6 VOCABULARY

🔊 1.10 Match the words with the pictures.

Then listen and check.

Word bank Possessions

an alarm clock	☐	an MP3 player	☐
a bottle of water	☐	a packet of tissues	☐
a calculator	☐	a passport	☐
a comb	☐	a pen	☐
a digital camera	☐	a photograph	☐
an ID card	☐	a ticket	☐
a key	☐	an umbrella	☐
a mobile phone	☐	a wallet	☐

7 LISTENING

🔊 1.11 Listen. What is in Adam's bag?

8 SPEAKING

Touch the pictures in exercise 6. Ask and answer.

A What's this?
B It's a/an _____.
A How do you spell it?
B _____

Now point at things in your classroom. Ask and answer.

A What's that called?
B It's a/an _____.
A How do you spell it?
B _____

9 WRITING

Write sentences about your three favourite things.

> **My three favourite things … Teresa**
> My MP3 player — with all my favourite songs on it.
> My cat — her name is Suzi.
> My bicycle — it's a present from my parents.

Extension Ask other students about their favourite things.

> What are your three favourite things?

LANGUAGE WORKOUT

Complete.

this/that
This is my favourite bag.
What's _____ in English?

That's a great bag.
_____'s my rucksack over there.

Indefinite article + singular nouns
a bag   **an** alarm clock
a passport   **an** ID card

▶**Answers and Practice**
Language File page 114

2 How old is it?

Telling the time
Describing places
these/those
Plural nouns
Questions: *How old ...?*
When ...?

1 OPENER

Who are the people in the photo?

His/Her name is …

2 READING

🔘 1.12 Read the dialogue. What is Katya pointing at?

MR WARD Right, here are maps of Brighton for our visitors, and these are copies of the programme for today.

KATYA Thank you very much. Emily, where are we on the map, please?

EMILY We're near the beach, here, next to the Royal Pavilion – this building here.

KATYA Wow, it's beautiful! How old is it?

EMILY I think it's about 200 years old.

KATYA Oh! And look at all those bicycles!

EMILY Yes, it's the London to Brighton Bike Ride today – with 25,000 people.

MR WARD Listen, everyone! Lunch is at half past twelve and …

ADAM Great! It's twenty-five past twelve now!

KATYA Excuse me, Mr Ward, when's the welcome party?

MR WARD It's on the programme – the party is at quarter to seven tonight. OK? Now, lunch everyone?

ADAM Yes, please!

STUDENT EXCHANGE

Today's programme

12.30	Welcome lunch
1.55	School visit
2.15	Film of Brighton
3.00	Tour of the city
6.45	Welcome party
8.30	Disco

3 AFTER READING

True or false? Correct the false sentences.

1 The students are in the Royal Pavilion.
2 The Royal Pavilion is two thousand years old.
3 The number of people in the Bike Ride is about twenty thousand.
4 Lunch is at 12.30.
5 The welcome party is at 7.15.

Your response Which is the best activity on the programme?

4 VOCABULARY

Complete.

Word Bank	Numbers		
20	twenty	80	eighty
21	twenty-one	90	_____
25	_____	100	a/one hundred
30	thirty	200	two hundred
40	forty	500	_____
50	fifty	1,000	a/one thousand
60	six___	2,000	_____ thousand
70	seven___	10,000	_____

🔘 1.13 Now listen and check. Repeat the numbers.

5 PRONUNCIATION

🔘 1.14 Listen and write the numbers you hear.

(thirty) *30*

6 LISTENING

🔘 1.15 Listen and match the watches with the people.

Jake Katya Adam Emily

Now listen and write the times you hear.

1 *12.40*

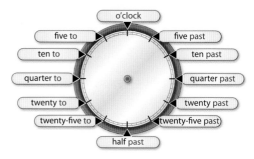

7 SPEAKING

Ask and answer questions about the times on the watches.

A Jake, what time is it, please?
B It's half past twelve.

Now look at the Student Exchange programme on page 14. Ask and answer.

A When's the welcome lunch?
B It's at half past twelve.

8 READING

🔘 1.16 Look at *Famous Places* and match the photos with the descriptions 1–4. Then listen and check.

Now ask and answer.

Where is Aya Sofya?   How old is it?

Word Bank Prepositions of place

in   on   next to   near

▶ Language File page 115

9 WRITING

Write a description of three buildings in your country.

What are their names? Where are they? How old are they?

Extension Read out your descriptions, but don't say the names of the buildings. Can other students guess what they are?

Famous Places

The Taj Mahal

The city of Machu Picchu

The temple of Abu Simbel

Aya Sofya

1 It's in Egypt next to the River Nile. It's 3,200 years old.
2 It's in the centre of Istanbul in Turkey. It's 1,500 years old.
3 It's near Delhi in India. It's 370 years old.
4 It's on a mountain in Peru. It's 550 years old.

LANGUAGE WORKOUT

Complete.

these/those
Singular this th__t   **Plural** th__se those

Plural nouns
+ **s**   bicycle**s** map**s** visitor__ year__
+ **es**   address**es** watch__
− **y** + **ies** city – cit**ies** copy – cop__ party – part__
Irregular person – **people**

▶**Answers and Practice**
Language File page 114

NICE TO MEET YOU

When's your birthday?

Talking about your family
Possessive adjectives

1 OPENER

Find the pairs in the Word Bank.

> **Word Bank** Family
>
> brother   daughter   father   grandfather
> grandmother   husband   mother   sister
> son   wife

> brother

> sister

2 READING

1.17 Read the description of Katya's family. Match the names with the people in the photo.

back to album

Katya Petrova

< prev   my family   next >

This is a photo of my family. My mother is on the right –
her name is Valentina. It's her fortieth birthday today.
I can't believe she's 40! The man next to Mum is my father.
His name is Maxim and he's 42. My sister Anna is on the
left and she's 18. The boy in the orange T-shirt is my brother
– he's called Dima. The two people in the centre are my
grandparents, Vera and Mikhail. Mum is their daughter.
I'm not in the picture – I'm the family photographer!

submit caption

3 AFTER READING

Match the questions with the answers.

1 How old is Valentina?
2 Is her birthday today?
3 Are Katya and Anna sisters?
4 Is Dima the boyfriend of Anna?
5 Is Katya the daughter of Dima?
6 What is the name of the grandmother?
7 Who is the son of Maxim and Valentina?
8 Who is the family photographer?

a No, she's his sister.
b She's 40.
c Dima.
d Katya.
e No, he's her brother.
f Yes, they are.
g Vera.
h Yes, it is.

Your response What are the people in your family called?

4 VOCABULARY

Match the numbers with the words.

> **Word Bank** Ordinal numbers
>
> 1st   2nd   3rd   4th   5th   6th
> 7th   8th   9th   10th   11th
> 12th   13th   14th   15th   16th
> 17th   18th   19th   20th   21st
> 22nd ...   30th   31st ...   40th
>
> twelfth   thirtieth   eighth   third
> nineteenth   seventh   twenty-first
> tenth   first   fourteenth   sixth
> fortieth   fifteenth   twenty-second
> fourth   second   twentieth
> seventeenth   eleventh   thirty-first
> sixteenth   ninth   fifth   thirteenth
> eighteenth

1.18 Listen and check. Repeat the numbers.

Extension Play *Number Tennis*.

> Three.

> Third!

5 PRONUNCIATION

🔘 1.19 Listen and mark the stress.

> **Word Bank** Months of the year
>
> January February March April
> May June July August September
> October November December

■
January

Now listen again and repeat.

6 LISTENING

🔘 1.20 Listen and write the birthdays.

1 *21st August*

Now point at the people. Ask and answer.

> When's his birthday?

> It's on the twenty-first of August.

> When's your birthday?

7 SPEAKING

Ask other students questions about their families.

> How old is your father?

> When's his birthday?

8 WRITING

Complete Katya's family tree.

The Petrova Family

grandfather Mikhail — Vera _____

_____ Maxim — Valentina _____

_____ Anna **Katya** Dima _____

> **Extension** Draw a family tree for another student.

LANGUAGE WORKOUT

Complete.

Personal pronouns	Possessive adjectives
I	_____
_____	your
he/_____/it	_____/her/its
_____	our
you	_____
they	_____

▶ **Answers and Practice**
Language File page 115

Personal information

FI WELCOME TO THE NEW FRIENDS INTERNATIONAL WEBSITE

- Home
- New Friends International
- Exchanges
- Programme
- Photos
- Noticeboard
- Chatroom

Hi! I'm Teresa Navarro and I'm from Valencia in Spain. Here's a picture of Valencia – it's a great city. I'm 15 years old and my birthday is in April – it's on 22nd April. Rihanna is my favourite singer.

Hello, I'm Pierre. My surname is Dubois and I'm from Geneva in Switzerland. Here's a picture of Geneva – it's very beautiful. I'm 14 years old and my birthday is on 2nd September. My favourite singer is Beyoncé.

Hi everyone. I'm Katya Petrova and I'm Russian, from Moscow. It's a great place – here's a picture. I'm 15 and my birthday is on 20th February. My favourite singer is Mika.

1 OPENER

Guess: Where are the places in the photos?

READING

2 🔘 1.21 Complete the questions with *How, What, Where, When, Who.* Then read the information on the New Friends International website and answer the questions for Teresa, Pierre and Katya.

1 _____ is her/his surname?
2 _____ is her/his nationality?
3 _____ is she/he from?
4 _____ old is she/he?
5 _____ is her/his birthday?
6 _____ is her/his favourite singer?

3 Here are Jake's answers to the questions in exercise 2. Match the questions with the answers.

11th March   Washington DC   Turner
Jay-Z   14   American

4 LISTENING

🔘 1.22 Listen to Emily and Adam and complete.

First name	Emily
Surname	
Nationality	
Age	
Birthday	
Favourite singer	

First name	Adam
Surname	
Nationality	
Age	
Birthday	
Favourite singer	

5 SPEAKING

Interview three other students and complete this form for them.

First name	
Surname	
Nationality	
Age	
Birthday	
Favourite singer	

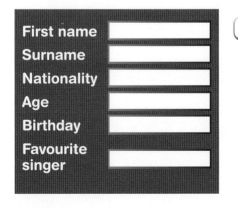

What's your ...?

How old are you?

6 WRITING

Look at the information about Teresa, Pierre and Katya on the website. Use the interviews in exercise 5 to write sentences about three students.

Her name is ...

LEARNER INDEPENDENCE

7 🔘 1.23 Classroom English: Listen and repeat.

What's this/that?
What's it called?
What's the English word for ...?
What's ... in English?
How do you spell it?
Sorry, I don't understand.
How do you pronounce
  F-E-B-R-U-A-R-Y?
What does ... mean?

8 Start a vocabulary notebook with these sections.

Telling the time
Family
Months of the year
Classroom English

FAMILY

Male	Female
grandfather	grandmother
uncle	aunt

9 🔘 1.24 **Phrasebook:** Find these useful expressions in Unit 1. Then listen and repeat.

Hello.   Hi.   Sorry?
Oh, I see.   Guess!
OK.   Right!
Thank you very much.
Wow!   Great!
Excuse me.   Yes, please.

Now write a three-line dialogue using one or more of the expressions.

A *Excuse me, what's your name?*
B *Angelina Jolie.*
A *Wow! It's nice to meet you.*

LANGUAGE LINKS

International words in English

How many of these words can you see on signs in your town?

SKETCH *Back To Front*

🔘 1.26 Read and listen.

A Excuse me.
B Yes?
A What time is it, please?
B It's nine past twenty.
A Sorry? Nine past twenty?
B Yes, that's right. Nine past twenty.
A Oh. And what month is it, please?
B Month? It's Lirpa, of course.
A Sorry, I don't understand. What does Lirpa mean?
B Lirpa? It's the month next to Yam.
A Oh! Where are you from?
B Here, of course.
A And where's here?
B Where we are now. Here is here and there is over there.
A And what's here called?
B Kcab.
A Sorry, how do you spell that?
B T-H-A-T.
A No, the name of this place.
B K-C-A-B.
A What?
B Kcab. Here everything is back to front!

Now act out the sketch in pairs.

Game WORD BINGO

Look at the pictures and choose nine things.
Write the words on the Bingo card.

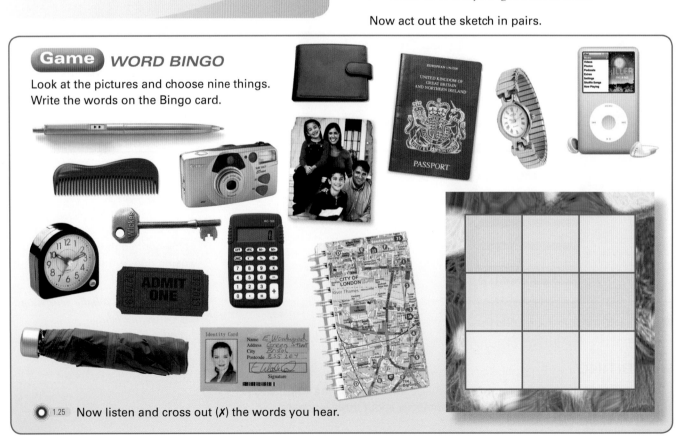

🔘 1.25 Now listen and cross out (✗) the words you hear.

REVISION

LESSON 1   Write the names of these things. Use *a/an*.

A   *a bottle of water*

LESSON 2   Write the times.

A   *It's half past three.*

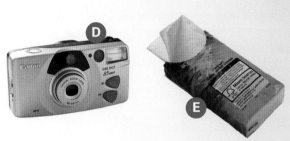

LESSON 3   Look at the photo of Katya's family on page 16. Write about all the people in the photo.

That's her sister on the left. Her name is Anna and she's 18.

LESSON 4   Write sentences about Emily and Adam using the information in exercise 4 on page 19.

Emily
Her surname is Fry.

EXTENSION

LESSON 1   Write the names of things in your bag.

LESSON 2   Write questions and answers about famous places in your country.

Where's the Colosseum?
It's in the centre of Rome.
How old is it?
I think it's about 2,000 years old.

LESSON 3   Find a photo of your family. Write about all the people in the photo, and give their names and ages.

That's my mother on the right. Her name is ...

LESSON 4   Look at the information about Pierre and Katya on page 18. Write similar information about your best friend.

My best friend is called ...

YOUR CHOICE!

HOW DO YOU SPELL IT?

- Work in pairs.
- Ask each other to spell words from Unit 1.

  A How do you spell 'bicycle'?

  B B-I-C-Y-C-L-E.

  A That's right!

COUNT AND CLAP

- Work in a small group.
- Choose a number from 3–10, for example 5. Start counting round the group, but when you get to 5, 10, 15, 20, etc, don't say the number – clap your hands or snap your fingers instead:

  1 2 3 4 *clap* 6 7 8 9 *clap* 11 12 13 14 *clap* …

COUNTRIES AROUND THE WORLD

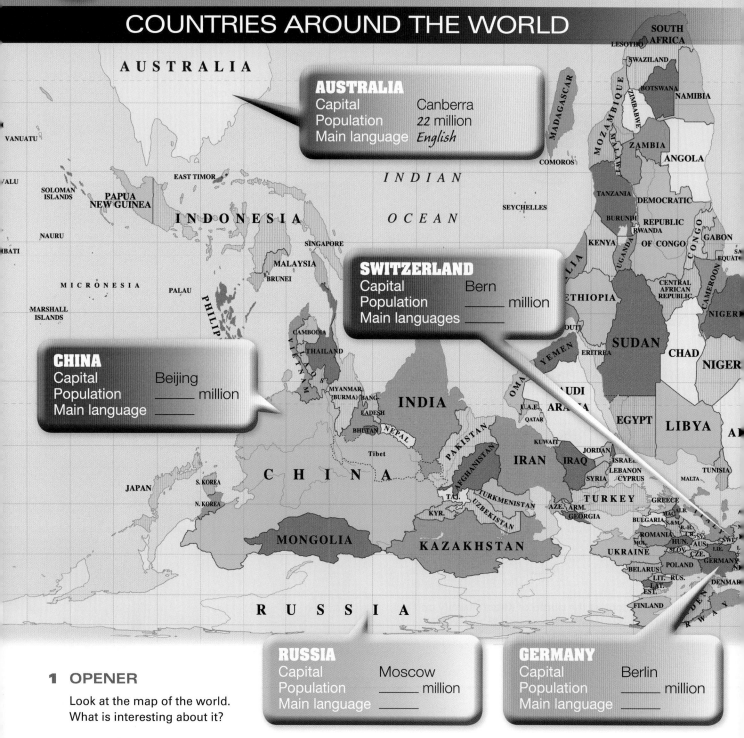

AUSTRALIA
Capital   Canberra
Population   22 million
Main language   *English*

SWITZERLAND
Capital   Bern
Population   _____ million
Main languages   _____

CHINA
Capital   Beijing
Population   _____ million
Main language   _____

RUSSIA
Capital   Moscow
Population   _____ million
Main language   _____

GERMANY
Capital   Berlin
Population   _____ million
Main language   _____

1 OPENER

Look at the map of the world.
What is interesting about it?

2 LISTENING

🔘 1.27 Listen and complete the country boxes with this information.

Population
8 million   22 million   34 million   46 million
82 million   111 million   142 million
193 million   310 million   1,340 million

Languages
Chinese   English   French   German   Italian
Portuguese   Russian   Spanish

3 PRONUNCIATION

🔘 1.28 Listen and repeat the countries and languages. Mark the stress.

■
Australia

4 SPEAKING

Ask and answer questions about the countries.

What's the capital of Germany?

What's the population of Russia?

What are the main languages in the USA?

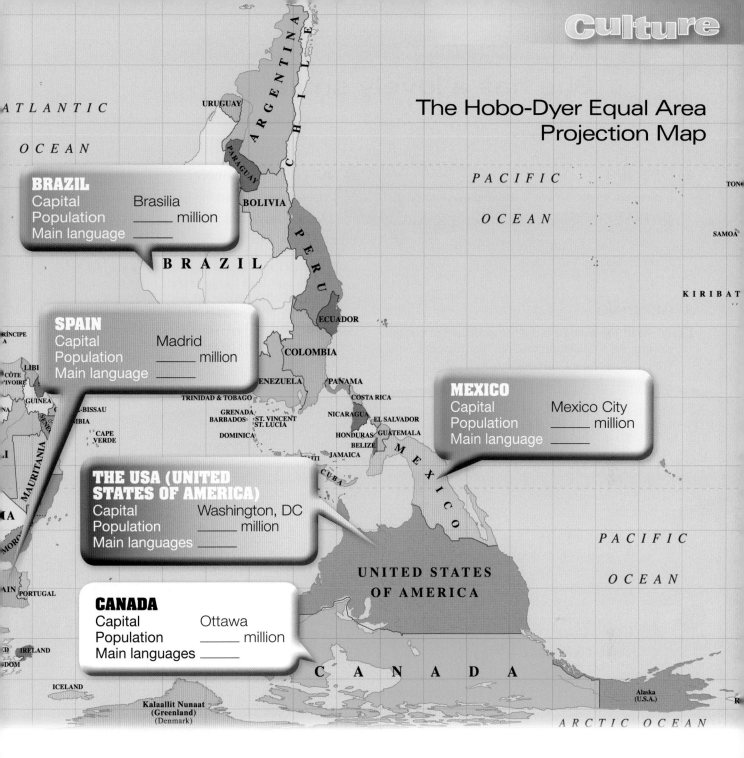

The Hobo-Dyer Equal Area Projection Map

BRAZIL
Capital   Brasilia
Population   _____ million
Main language _____

SPAIN
Capital   Madrid
Population   _____ million
Main language _____

MEXICO
Capital   Mexico City
Population   _____ million
Main language _____

THE USA (UNITED STATES OF AMERICA)
Capital   Washington, DC
Population   _____ million
Main languages _____

CANADA
Capital   Ottawa
Population   _____ million
Main languages _____

---

5 LISTENING

 Listen and say where the music is from.

Number one.   It's Mexican.

6 WRITING

Write about five of the countries.

The capital of Australia is Canberra and the population is 22 million. The main language is English.

7 MINI-PROJECT
Countries around the world

Work with another student and find out information to complete boxes for five more countries.

COUNTRY
Capital   _____
Population   _____ million
Main language(s) _____

Now join other students and put your information together.

2 1

She has a lovely smile

Describing people
have: **affirmative**

1 OPENER

Look at the magazine article and find these colours.

Word Bank Colours

black   blue   brown   green   grey   orange
pink   purple   red   white   yellow

2 READING

1.30 Read *Teenagers around the world* and match the paragraphs 1–5 with photos A–E. Then look at the flags. Which countries are the people from?

3 AFTER READING

True or false? Correct the false sentences.

1 Laxmi has a red sari.
2 Daniel has black shoes.
3 Kumiko has blue hair.
4 Laxmi's and Hanna's flags have three colours.
5 The boys with hats have black trousers.
6 Daniel's flag has five colours.

Your response What do you think of the clothes in the photos?

TEENAGERS AROUND THE WORLD

1 Laxmi has long dark hair and brown eyes. Her red sari is nine metres long. She has a lovely smile. Her country's flag has three colours: orange, white and green.

Germany

Japan

India

2 Daniel has a green T-shirt, long grey shorts and long red socks. He has white shoes – and a football. His country's flag has lots of colours: black, green, yellow, red, white and blue.

3 Kumiko has pink hair and big sunglasses. Her T-shirt is black, her trousers are red check, and she has a shoulder bag. Her country's flag has two colours: red and white.

5 Hanna has long blonde hair and blue eyes. Her top is purple, and her trousers and sandals are red. She has a long scarf round her neck. Her country's flag is black, red and yellow.

4 Pedro and **Felipe** have short black hair. They have white shirts, black trousers and black shoes. They also have white hats. Their country's flag is red, white and blue.

D

South Africa

Puerto Rico

A

B

C

E

4 VOCABULARY

What are the three people wearing? Choose from these words.

> **Word Bank** Clothes
>
> cap hat jacket jeans pullover sandals
> scarf shirt shoes shorts skirt socks
> top trainers trousers

> Number 1 is a shirt.

> I think number 2 is a pair of trousers.

🔘 1.31 Listen and check.

5 LISTENING

🔘 1.32 Listen and complete the chart.

	Teresa	Pierre	Katya	Jake
cap				
jacket	1			
pair of jeans	3			
pullover				
shirt				
pair of shoes				
skirt				
top				
pair of trainers				

Now talk about the students' clothes.

> Teresa has a jacket and three pairs of jeans.

> **Extension** Play *Who is it?* Describe people in the photos on page 24.

> She has red trousers and a purple top.

> Hanna!

6 PRONUNCIATION

🔘 1.33 Listen and repeat.

/ð/ they	/θ/ think
there	three
then	thanks
father	birthday
clothes	fourth

Now listen and write these words under *they* or *think*.

> brother mother month thing third those

7 SPEAKING

🔘 1.34 Look at the picture and listen. Identify these stars.

Tara Tress Oscar Oldman Rosie Raven Peter Punk
Holly Hyde Max Minster

Now describe the stars.

> Which one is Tara Tress?

> She has long blonde hair and blue eyes.

8 WRITING

Write a paragraph of an email to a new friend describing yourself and people in your family.

**I have red hair and green eyes.
My brother has …**

> ### LANGUAGE WORKOUT
>
> Complete.
>
> *have*
> **Affirmative**
> I/you/we/they **have**
> he/she/it **has**
>
> They _____ black trousers.
> He _____ a football.
> She _____ long blonde hair.
>
> ►**Answers and Practice**
> Language File page 115

2
2
I can play the guitar

Talking about ability
can and *can't*
Linking words: *and, but, or*

1 OPENER

Which of these can you see in the photo?

> an alarm clock   a bed   books   a guitar
> jeans   a light switch   a mobile phone
> a photo   a piano   a red cap
> a rucksack   a saxophone   shoes

2 READING

🔘 1.35   Read the dialogue and find five different languages.

EMILY   Here's your room.

TERESA   It's really nice, Emily. And what's this? Can you play the saxophone?

EMILY   Yes, I can. … How's that?

TERESA   Fantastic! I can't play an instrument, but I can sing. What other instruments can you play?

EMILY   I can play the guitar and the piano – but not at the same time as the sax!

TERESA   Great – we can have a two-girl band. We can sing in lots of languages – English, Spanish, German …

EMILY   Oh dear, I can speak French and a little Italian, but I can't speak Spanish or German.

TERESA   Never mind! I can sing in Spanish and you can sing in English.

EMILY   OK. Now can I help you with anything? Any questions?

TERESA   Yes, it's silly, but I can't find the light switch.

EMILY   It's over here behind the door. See?

TERESA   No, I can't see! Now it's dark!

3 AFTER READING

Match the questions with the answers. There is one wrong answer.

1   Who can't play an instrument?
2   Can Emily and Teresa speak English?
3   Who can't speak Spanish?
4   Who can speak French?
5   Where's the light switch?

a   Yes, they can.
b   Emily can.
c   Emily can't.
d   It's behind the door.
e   Teresa is silly.
f   Teresa can't.

Your response Can you play an instrument?

4 PRONUNCIATION

🔘 1.36 Listen and repeat.

> **Weak form:** /kən/
> She can play the guitar.
> Who can speak French?
> **Strong forms:** /kæn/ and /kɑːnt/
> Yes, I can.
> No, I can't.
> I can't play the guitar.

Now listen and decide: weak or strong?

1 We can sing in lots of languages.
2 I can't see.
3 Yes, I can.
4 What can you play?

5 SPEAKING

Do the Life Skills Questionnaire. Then compare your answers with two other students.

> **Extension** Play *Find someone who can ... .*
> Ask other students the questions in the Life Skills Questionnaire. The winner is the first with 12 *Yes, I can* answers.

LIFE SKILLS QUESTIONNAIRE
How are your twenty-first century life skills?

1 Can you programme a satnav?

2 Can you send photos from a mobile?

3 Can you burn a CD?

4 Can you create a web page?

5 Can you download music?

6 Can you use a social networking site?

And how are your other life skills?

7 Can you mend a bicycle puncture?

8 Can you cook a meal?

9 Can you iron a shirt?

10 Can you run a kilometre in five minutes?

11 Can you swim underwater?

12 Can you ride a horse?

6 WRITING

Make your own Life Skills Questionnaire about these topics.

Memory   tell jokes? remember people's names? remember dates and places?

Music   sing? read music? dance?

Hands   draw a picture? paint a wall? make a cake? sew on a button?

Strength   lift 20 kilos? swim 100 metres? walk on your hands?

Now give your questionnaire to five students. Write a paragraph about the answers.

> **Extension** Complete your own Life Skills Questionnaire for a member of your family. Are their answers the same as yours?

LANGUAGE WORKOUT

Complete.

can and ***can't***

Affirmative	**Negative**
I **can** play the guitar.	I **can't** speak Spanish.
She _____ sing.	She _____ play the piano.

Questions	**Short answers**
Can you play the sax?	Yes, I/we _____. / No, I/we **can't**.
_____ they sing?	Yes, they **can**. / No, they _____.

Contraction _____ = cannot

Linking words: *and, but, or*
I can play the guitar _____ the piano.
I can't play an instrument, _____ I can sing.
I can't speak Spanish _____ German.

▶**Answers and Practice**
Language File pages 115–116

Keep still

Giving instructions
Imperatives
Definite article

Video Call User Guide
Choose your problem

- **The picture isn't great**
  Make sure your webcam is on.
  Keep still and don't move around.
  Check there's light on your face
  – don't sit with your back to a
  window.

- **The sound isn't great**
  Go to Menu, select Audio and
  check the microphone and
  speakers.
  Don't speak a long way from the
  microphone.

1 OPENER

This lesson is about video calls and phone calls. Guess:
Which of these words are in the lesson?

code   computer   dial   father   hair   jeans   menu
microphone   number   select   swim   webcam

2 READING

🔘 1.37 Read the dialogue and the User Guide. What's Pierre's problem and
what's the solution?

PIERRE Wow! Your school has really good computers.
ADAM   Yes, that's a new laptop.
PIERRE Lucky you! Can I make a video call to my family in Switzerland?
ADAM   Yes, of course you can.
PIERRE Adam – there's something wrong. I can see my mum but she can't see
       me. The picture isn't very good.
ADAM   Don't worry – look at the User Guide.
PIERRE OK … the User Guide is open.
ADAM   Now check the webcam.
PIERRE The webcam is on.
ADAM   Right – so it isn't the webcam. But there's no light on your face. Come
       and sit over here with the laptop.
PIERRE Hey, the picture's great now! Thanks a lot.
ADAM   No problem. Say hello to your mum from me.

3 AFTER READING

True or false? Correct the false
sentences.

1 For a good picture, make sure
  there is no light on your face.
2 To check the sound, go to Menu
  and select Audio.
3 Don't speak near the microphone.
4 Pierre has a new laptop.
5 Pierre can see and talk to his
  mother in Switzerland.

Your response Is there a
webcam on a computer at your
school or at home? Can you make
video calls?

4 LISTENING

🔘 1.38 Listen to Katya and Mrs Fry, Emily's mother. Tick (✔) what Mrs Fry says.

1 ☐ Use your mobile.
  ☐ Don't use your mobile.

2 ☐ You can use our phone.
  ☐ You can't use our phone.

3 ☐ First, dial the international code.
  ☐ First, dial the national code.

4 ☐ Dial 006.
  ☐ Dial 007.

5 ☐ Dial the first number of the area code.
  ☐ Don't dial the first number of the area code.

6 ☐ Then dial your parents' number.
  ☐ Then dial your number.

Extension Tell each other how to make a call from Britain to your home.

5 PRONUNCIATION

🔘 1.39 Listen and write these words in the correct column.

about   address   around   hello   menu
message   mobile   number   parent   picture
select   today   tonight   webcam

■ ▪	▪ ■
menu	*about*

Now listen and check. Repeat the words.

READING

6 Match the text message abbreviations with the words.

UR = you are   **2B** = to be   **THX** = thanks

```
2DAY  2MORO
ABT  B4N  BF  CU
EZ  GF  GR8  IC
ILUVU  L8  L8R
2NITE  NE  PLS
RUOK  SOME1
```

about   any   are you OK?
boyfriend   bye for now
easy   girlfriend   great   late
later   I love you   I see
please   see you   someone
today   tomorrow   tonight

7 Put these messages in the right order. A is the first one.

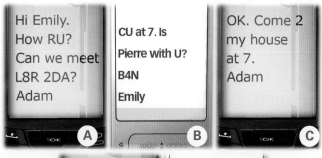

Hi Emily. How RU? Can we meet L8R 2DA? Adam **A**

CU at 7. Is Pierre with U? B4N Emily **B**

OK. Come 2 my house at 7. Adam **C**

Yes. He's GR8. CU L8R Adam **D**

Can't 2DA - what ABT 2MORO? Emily **E**

8 WRITING

Write out this text message in full.

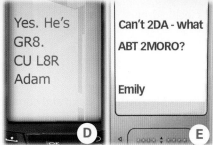

HI! THX 4 THE CD.
ILUV IT. RUOK?
CU 2MORO ABT 6.
PLS DNT B L8
B4N

Hi! Thanks ...

LANGUAGE WORKOUT

Complete.

Imperatives
Go to Menu.   **Keep** still.
_____ the microphone.
Don't move around.
_____ sit with your back to a window.

Contraction

_____ = do not

We use the imperative to give instructions.

Definite article
Dial **the** international code.
What's **the** number?
Check **the** microphone.

▶**Answers and Practice**
Language File page 116

Favourite band

1 OPENER

This lesson is about bands. Guess: Which of these words are in the lesson?

CDs   clock   drums   friends   gigs   guitar
horse   jacket   members   song   website

2 READING

🔘 1.40   Read *My Favourite Band* and complete the questionnaire for Jake.

Jake

What's your favourite band?
Linkin Park

How many members are there?

Where are they from?

What's your favourite song?

What's special about the band?

What's their website address?

What's on the website?

MY FAVOURITE BAND

Jake

'My favourite band is Linkin Park. It has six members and they're from California, in the USA. The band is called Linkin Park after Lincoln Park in Santa Monica, California. I have all their CDs – my favourite song is called *Leave Out All the Rest*.

A special thing about the band: three of the members – Rob, Brad and Mike – are school friends. Rob plays the drums, Brad plays the guitar and Mike raps.

Their website is www.linkinpark.com and it's really cool. It has some fantastic pictures of the band, and you can also download videos of their gigs.'

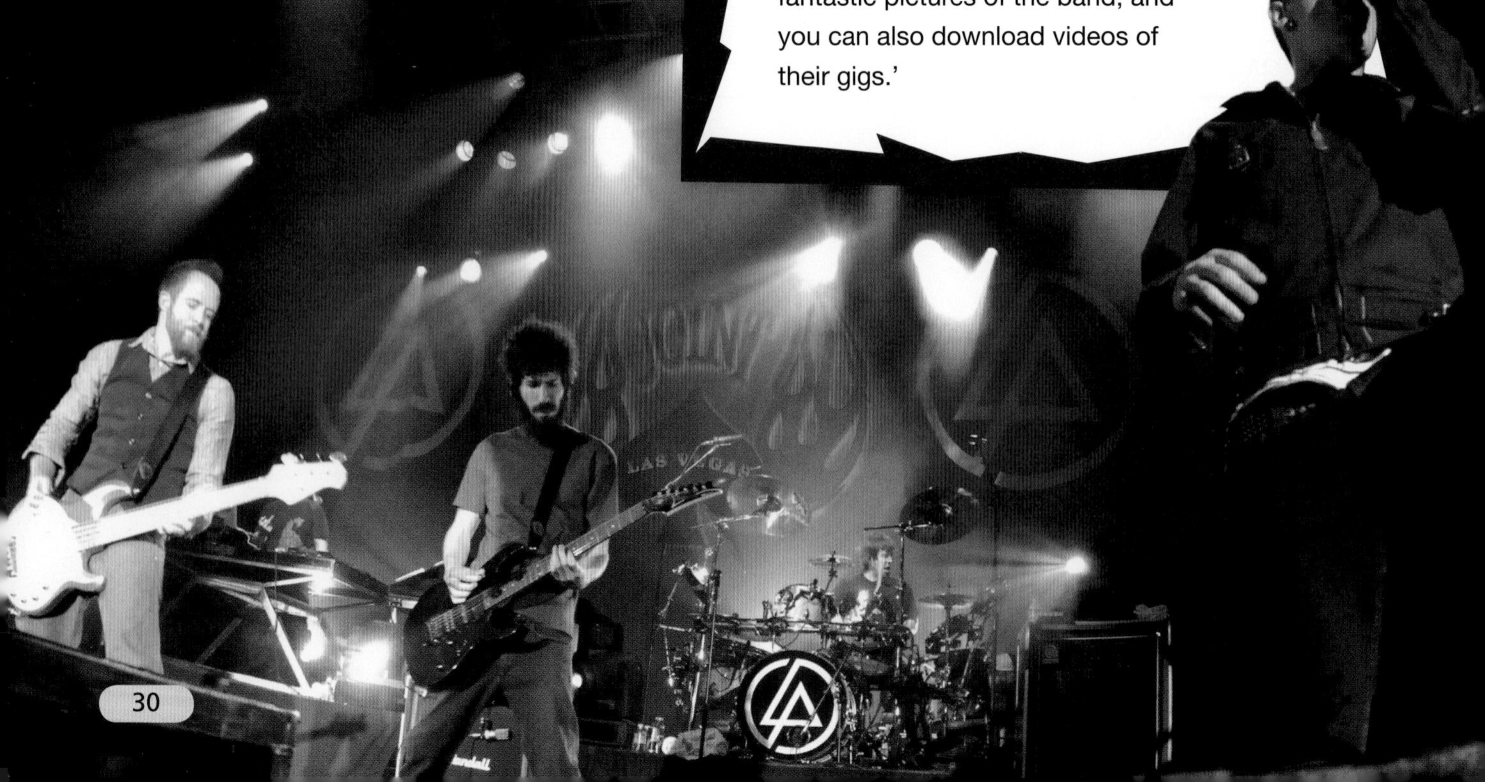

LEARNER INDEPENDENCE

6 Classroom English: Ask and answer.

Making requests

Excuse me, can I …
    ask a question,
    open a window,
    close the door,
    borrow your book,   please?
    leave the room,
    get a drink of water,
    go to the toilet,
    go home,

> Yes, of course you can.

> No, I'm sorry, you can't.

Now make and reply to requests about these things.

> bag   bicycle   calculator
> dictionary   mobile
> pen   umbrella   watch

> Can I borrow your …?

> Yes, of course you can.

> No, I'm sorry. It's at home.

7 Add these sections to your vocabulary notebook.

Clothes   Musical instruments

8 🔘 1.42 **Phrasebook:** Find these useful expressions in Unit 2. Then listen and repeat.

> Never mind!
> Any questions?
> See?   Lucky you!
> Yes, of course you can.
> There's something wrong.
> Don't worry.
> Thanks a lot.
> No problem.
> It's really cool.

Which expression:

a   is a reply to a request?
b   means that there's a problem?
c   means that you like something very much?
d   is a reply to 'Thanks a lot.'?

Emily

What's your favourite band?
Black Eyed Peas

How many members are there?

Where are they from?

What's your favourite song?

What's special about the band?

What's their website address?

What's on the website?

---

3 LISTENING

🔘 1.41 Listen to Emily talking about her favourite band and complete the questionnaire.

4 SPEAKING

Ask two other students about their favourite bands. Use the questions in the questionnaire and write down the answers.

> What's your favourite band?

5 WRITING

Use your notes from exercise 4 to write a paragraph about another student's favourite band. Use the text in exercise 2 to help you.

PROJECT
Personal web page

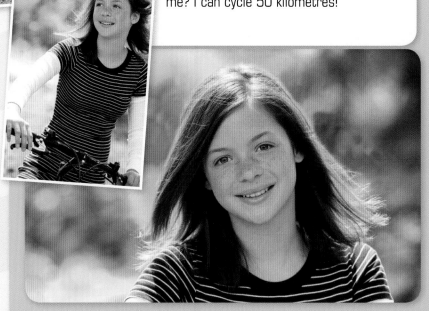

Hi!
My name's Merel and I'm 14. My birthday's on 20th January. I have two brothers, Wim and Pieter. Wim's 12 and Pieter's 15. I'm from Antwerp in Belgium. I have lots of friends at school and my best friend is Saskia. My favourite clothes are jeans and my pink pullover. My favourite things are my bicycle and my dog, Pluto. My favourite band is the indie group, Florence and the Machine. I can play the guitar and speak three languages: Dutch, French and English. Something special about me? I can cycle 50 kilometres!

1 Make a list of information to include in your personal web page, for example:

Name Age Birthday Family
Where you live   Friends
Favourite clothes and colours
Favourite band/singer
Favourite kind of music
Favourite things
Things you can do
Something special about you

2 Write the text for your web page, read it carefully and correct any mistakes.

3 Design your web page. Draw pictures and add photos. Show your personal web page to other students.

Game *NOUGHTS AND CROSSES*

- Form two teams: Team O and Team X.
- Teams take turns to choose a square. They say and spell a word in the category, for example:
  Colours – blue, B-L-U-E.
- A correct answer wins the square for that team – O or X.
- The first team to get a line of three Os or three Xs in any direction wins the game.

Colours	Clothes	Family
Countries	Music	Languages
Possessive adjectives	Months	Mobile phones

Puzzle

Read and find the word.

You can find my first in *good* and in *game*
My second is in *number* but it isn't in *name*
My third is in *sing* but it isn't in *song*
My fourth is in *right* but it isn't in *wrong*
My fifth is in *cap* and *jacket* and *jeans*
My sixth is in *red* and *brown* and *green*
My whole is something you can play
What's the word – can you say?

REVISION

LESSON 1 Write eight words for colours.

Colours   *green*

LESSON 2 Make a list of action verbs.

swim, ride, ...

Now write true sentences with *can* and *can't* and action verbs.

I can swim 1,000 metres.
I can't ride a moped.

LESSON 3 Make a list of words about using a phone.

dial, international code, ...

LESSON 4 Look at the completed questionnaire in exercise 3 on page 31 and write a paragraph about Emily's favourite band. Use the text about Linkin Park to help you.

EXTENSION

LESSON 1 Choose photos of people in *New Inspiration 1*. Write short descriptions of the people.

Katya has an orange top, blue jeans and white shoes.

LESSON 2 Write an interview between you and a famous person. Ask what he/she can and can't do.

Tell me, Johnny, can you dance?
No, I can't.

LESSON 3 Write instructions and commands you can hear in your English class.

Open your books.
Don't use mobile phones in class.

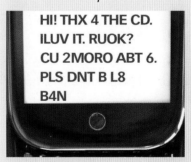

HI! THX 4 THE CD.
ILUV IT. RUOK?
CU 2MORO ABT 6.
PLS DNT B L8
B4N

LESSON 4 Write out a song by your favourite band with some words missing. Ask another student to listen to the song and complete the words.

YOUR CHOICE!

STAR PROFILE

- Write a profile of your favourite star (film, music or sport). Think about:
  Birthday   Hair and eyes   Favourite music
  Favourite clothes and colours   Something special
  Website
- Draw pictures or find photographs from magazines or the Internet for your profile.
- Show your Star Profile to another student.

DICTIONARY SEARCH

- Use two dictionaries – an English-English dictionary and a bilingual dictionary.
- Look up words for clothes in the bilingual dictionary.
- Find definitions of the same words in the English-English dictionary and write them down.
- Show the definitions to another student and ask them to guess the words.
- Add the new words to the *Clothes* section of your vocabulary notebook.

1 Read and complete. For each number 1–10, choose word A, B or C.

Mobile World

Lots of mobiles have cameras, so you can take ___1___ with your phone and send them to your friends. You ___2___ also make and download videos. And lots of mobiles ___3___ MP3 players too, so you can ___4___ to music by your ___5___ band.

In some countries phone calls from a mobile can ___6___ expensive, so people send ___7___ messages. Students can't have mobiles in UK school classrooms – they text each other with the answers to the teacher's ___8___!

With a smartphone you ___9___ also send email, surf the web and download apps (applications). So you can have Facebook, Flickr or YouTube on your ___10___, as well as games and e-books. And in the future? A mobile which can check how you are and call a doctor!

1	A places	B pictures	C numbers
2	A are	B can	C have
3	A are	B is	C be
4	A play	B sing	C listen
5	A silly	B lucky	C favourite
6	A is	B be	C are
7	A phone	B song	C text
8	A calls	B texts	C questions
9	A can	B has	C have
10	A phone	B computer	C website

2 Write questions and answers.

Pierre/14 ✓
Is Pierre 14? Yes, he is.
Pierre/15 ✗
Is Pierre 15? No, he isn't.

1 Emily/14 ✓
2 Jake/from Spain ✗
3 Adam and Emily/English ✓
4 Machu Picchu/in Switzerland ✗
5 Katya/from Russia ✓
6 Pierre/from Brighton ✗
7 Emily and Teresa/sisters ✗
8 October/the tenth month ✓

3 Complete the questions.

1 What _____ your _____?
   Teresa Navarro.
2 Where _____ you _____?
   Valencia in Spain.
3 How old _____ you?
   I'm fifteen.
4 What _____ your mum's name?
   Luisa.
5 Who _____ your favourite singers?
   Rihanna and Katy Perry.

4 Complete with *this*, *that*, *these* or *those*.

1 Is _____ your umbrella over there?
2 Emily, _____ is my friend Jake. – Nice to meet you.
3 Here are the maps, and _____ are copies of the programme.
4 Are _____ your bags over there?

5 Write the plural form of the nouns.

1	a friend	7	an address
2	a street	8	a family
3	a city	9	a month
4	a watch	10	a country
5	a person	11	a camera
6	a photo	12	a tissue

6 Complete with possessive adjectives.

1 Adam: 'This is _____ sister. _____ name is Ruby.'
2 Emily: 'Mr Ward is a teacher. _____ first name is David.'
3 Adam: 'Is that girl your friend? What's _____ name?'
4 Mr and Mrs Campbell: '_____ address is 8 Hill Street.'
5 Pierre: 'I have the Campbells' address, but what's _____ phone number?'
6 Teresa: 'I have a cat.' Emily: 'What's _____ name?'

7 Complete with the correct form of *have*.

1 He _____ two sisters.
2 I _____ a red phone.
3 They _____ brown hair.
4 We _____ two Russian friends.
5 My father _____ blue eyes.
6 She _____ black shoes.

8 Write questions and answers.

Jake/speak Russian ✗/speak Spanish ✓
Can Jake speak Russian? No, he can't.
Can he speak Spanish? Yes, he can.

1 Emily/play the guitar ✓/play the drums ✗
2 they/swim 5km ✗/run 5km ✓
3 Pierre/ride a horse ✓/iron a shirt ✗
4 you/send a text message on a mobile ✓/burn a CD on a mobile ✗
5 Katya/speak French ✗/understand French ✓
6 she/read a book ✓/read music ✗

9 Write requests beginning *Can I ...?*

You can use my phone.
Can I use your phone?

1 You can close the window.
2 You can phone your parents.
3 You can see the photos.
4 You can borrow my jacket.
5 You can listen to my MP3 player.
6 You can use my camera.

10 Complete with *Don't* where necessary.

Notes for Exchange Students

1 _____ remember to ask for help.

2 _____ phone your parents.

3 _____ use a mobile in class.

4 _____ listen to Mr Ward.

5 _____ sing in class.

6 _____ forget the welcome party!

VOCABULARY

11 Complete with these words.

address   birthday   favourite   meet
message   past   sister   surname

1 Anna is Katya's _____.
2 What's the time? – It's half _____ twelve.
3 It's nice to _____ you.
4 What's your name and _____?
5 This is her _____ bag.
6 Petrova is Katya's _____.
7 It's my _____ today.
8 He can send a text _____.

12 Match these words with their definitions.

bicycle   brother   century   clock
December   German   grandmother
January   London   population

1 Your mother's mother.
2 Opposite of *sister*.
3 The first month.
4 The twelfth month.
5 They speak this language in Switzerland.
6 It's the capital of England.
7 You can ride it.
8 One hundred years.
9 It tells you the time.
10 The number of people in a country.

13 Match the verbs in list A with the words and phrases in list B.

	A	B
1	cook	the drums
2	dial	home
3	go	a horse
4	iron	a joke
5	lift	a meal
6	play	your name
7	ride	a number
8	send	a shirt
9	spell	ten kilos
10	tell	a text message

14 Find the odd word.

1 hundred   button   thousand   million
2 trainers   jacket   shirt   pullover
3 clock   calculator   phone   umbrella
4 brown   new   pink   green
5 Spain   French   German   Italian
6 drum   camera   guitar   saxophone
7 mother   sister   brother   boyfriend
8 wallet   bag   comb   rucksack

LEARNER INDEPENDENCE
SELF ASSESSMENT

Look back at Welcome! and Lessons 1–3 in Units 1 and 2.

How good are you at …?	✓Fine	? Not sure
1 Introducing yourself and others Workbook pp2–5 exercises 1–6, and p12 exercise 1	☐	☐
2 Talking about possessions Workbook pp6–7 exercises 1–4 and p8 exercises 3 and 4	☐	☐
3 Telling the time Workbook p9 exercise 10	☐	☐
4 Describing places Workbook p9 exercise 7	☐	☐
5 Talking about your family Workbook pp10–11 exercises 1, 4 and 5	☐	☐
6 Describing people Workbook pp18–19 exercises 1 and 5	☐	☐
7 Talking about ability Workbook pp20–21 exercises 1–5	☐	☐
8 Giving instructions Workbook pp22–23 exercises 1–4	☐	☐

Not sure? Have a look at Language File pages 114–116 and do the Workbook exercise(s) again.

Now write an example for 1–8

1 This is my friend Pierre.

COMMUNICATIVE AIMS
LEARNING HOW TO ...

1 Talk about likes and dislikes
2 Talk about regular activities
3 Say how often you do things
4 Describe places and facilities
5 Describe what's happening now

TOPICS AND VOCABULARY

Food

Prepositions of time

School subjects

Days of the week

Sport and the gym

Leisure activities

Tourist attractions

Furniture and equipment

Parts of the body

1 Match the pictures (A–F) with six items in the Topics and Vocabulary box.

2 Put the words into categories.

| Food | Sport |

| Parts of the body |

cheese fish egg tomato football tennis ear leg basketball swimming eye hand mouth golf banana

Her face is really white!

A

B

Babar Ali's favourite subject is history.

3 Match the words with the pictures.

car   face   magazine   octopus   shop   volleyball

C

Don't miss the wonderful treasures of Tutankhamun.

F

I play computer games or listen to music in my free time.

Great! I like eggs.

D

5 Do the survey with three other students.
Can you find people who agree with you?

FOOD AND SPORT SURVEY

Do you like …?   ☺ = Yes!   ☺ = It's OK.   ☹ = No!

pizza

fish

salad

football

tennis

swimming

I usually start on the rowing machine.

E

4 ◯ 2.01 Listen to extracts 1–3 from Units 3 and 4.
Match them with these topics.

A   Leisure activities
B   Food
C   Tourist attractions

Believe it or not!

SWIMS is the longest English word which you can read upside down – try it!

I really don't like octopus

Talking about likes and dislikes
Present simple: affirmative and negative

1 OPENER

Who can you see in the photo? Where are they?

2 READING

2.02 Read the dialogue. What's for dinner?

PIERRE	I love your house!
ADAM	It's a cottage, really. It's quite small.
PIERRE	In Geneva we live in a flat in the city centre – we don't have a garden.
RUBY	Pierre, come and see our chickens!
PIERRE	You have chickens!
RUBY	Yes, you can have fresh eggs for breakfast!
PIERRE	Great! I like eggs.
ADAM	Ruby, go away!
RUBY	Don't speak to me like that!
ADAM	Pierre wants to talk to me. He doesn't want to see the chickens.
RUBY	Sometimes I hate you, Adam!
DIANA CAMPBELL	Stop it, you two. Come inside, everyone – dinner is ready. Pierre, I hope you like fish.
PIERRE	Yes, I love it. I like everything except octopus. I really don't like octopus.
DIANA	Don't worry – octopus isn't on the menu!

3 AFTER READING

Choose the correct word.

1 Adam lives in a flat/cottage.
2 Pierre doesn't live in a house/flat.
3 Pierre likes chickens/eggs.
4 Ruby is angry with Pierre/Adam.
5 Diana says 'Stop it' to Adam and Pierre/Ruby.
6 Pierre loves fish/octopus.

Your response Is there something you really don't like?

4 VOCABULARY

Match the words with the pictures.

> Number 1 is yellow – it's cheese.

Word Bank Food

bananas (*yellow*)   carrots (*orange*)   cheese (*yellow*)
chips (*brown*)   chocolate (*brown*)   cucumber (*green*)
eggs (*yellow and white*)   fish (*grey*)   garlic (*white*)
ice cream (*pink*)   mushrooms (*white*)   octopus (*pink*)
pizza (*yellow and red*)   tomatoes (*red*)

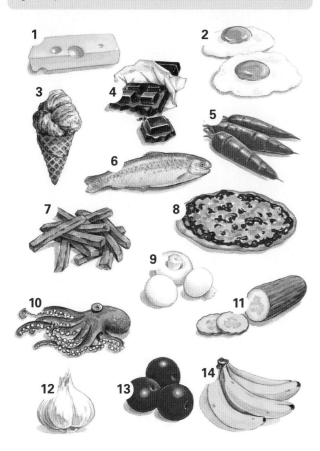

2.03 Now listen and check.

> **Extension** Say letters and food words.
> F   Fish.

5 PRONUNCIATION

Write the words in the correct column.

carrot   CD   centre   century   cheese   chicken
chip   chocolate   city   cottage   cream   cucumber

/tʃ/	/k/	/s/
cheese	*carrot*	*CD*

2.04 Now listen and check. Repeat the words.

6 LISTENING

2.05 Listen to Ruby and Adam and look at the pictures of food in exercise 4. Write the numbers of the things they like and don't like.

Ruby likes _____, _____
and _____.
She doesn't like _____,
_____ or _____.

Adam likes _____,
_____ and _____.
He doesn't like _____,
_____ or _____.

Now tell each other what they like and don't like.

7 SPEAKING

Tell each other about food you like and don't like.

> I like garlic, but I don't like fish or octopus.

> I love octopus, but I hate garlic!

8 WRITING

Do a survey: ask other students to tell you things they love, like, don't like and hate. They can talk about food, music, film stars …

Now write the results of your survey.

Ana loves hip-hop, but she doesn't like jazz.

> **Extension** Write about things you love, like, don't like and hate. Think about music, film stars, clothes, and colours.

LANGUAGE WORKOUT

Complete.

Present simple	
Affirmative	**Negative**
I like	I _____ like
you _____	you don't like
he/she/it like**s**	he/she/it _____ like
we like	we _____ like
they _____	they don't like

Contractions
_____ = do not   doesn't = does not

▶**Answers and Practice**
Language File pages 116–117

3 2 Does she study in the evening?

Talking about regular activities
Present simple: questions and short answers
Prepositions of time

1 OPENER

Look at the photos. What can you see? Where are the people?

2 READING

2.06 Read the magazine article. What information is surprising?

3 AFTER READING

Match the questions with the answers.

1 Does Babar Ali go to a school near his home?
2 Do hundreds of children go to Babar Ali's own school?
3 Do his students pay for books and meals?
4 Does the school have lots of classrooms?
5 Does the school teach the local language?
6 Does Babar Ali like history?
7 Does Chumki go to school for four hours a day?
8 Does she study in the evening?

a Yes, he does.
b No, he doesn't.
c Yes, she does.
d No, she doesn't.
e Yes, it does.
f No, it doesn't.
g Yes, they do.
h No, they don't.

Your response What do you think about Babar Ali's school?

Babar Ali, from West Bengal in India, is a student in the morning and a headmaster in the afternoon. At seven in the morning the 16-year-old goes to Raj Govinda school, ten kilometres from his home. But in the afternoon he is the headmaster of his own school for poor children, in the backyard of his home.

The school is free, and has 800 students aged 5–14, and ten teenage teachers. The children work in the fields or in people's houses in the morning and go to school in the afternoon. People give money to the school and the students don't pay for books or meals. Most of the classes are outdoors. The school teaches ten subjects, including Bengali (the local language), history, English, maths and geography. Babar Ali's favourite subject is history and he likes English.

Chumki Hajra, 14, is a student at Babar Ali's school. Every day she gets up at six and cleans people's houses all morning. At four o'clock she goes to Babar Ali's school. She comes home at seven after school and helps her parents. Before she goes to bed she studies with her brother and sister.

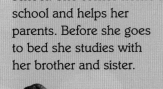

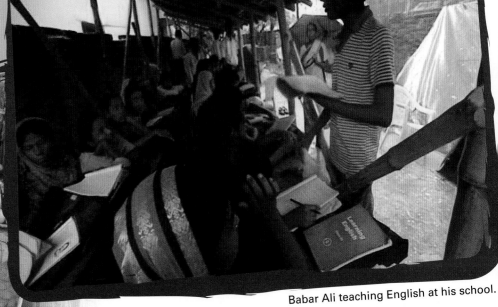

Babar Ali teaching English at his school.

4 LISTENING

🔘 2.07 Listen and complete Adam's school timetable.

	Monday	Tuesday	Wednesday	Thursday	Friday
9.00–10.05	Maths	Science	English	—	English
10.05–11.10	—	Computer studies	—	Geography	Science
BREAK					
11.30–12.05	Geography	—	History	English	Science
12.05–13.10	Art	Maths	German	German	—
LUNCH					
14.10–15.15	Science	Geography	PE (Physical Education)	Art	French

5 SPEAKING

Ask and answer questions about Adam's timetable.

A When does Adam have art?
B On Monday from five past twelve to ten past one, and on Thursday from ten past two to quarter past three.
A Does he have history on Tuesday?
B No, he doesn't.

Extension Compare your timetable with Adam's.
A Adam has geography on Thursday, but I have it on Wednesday.
B We both have computer studies on Tuesday.

Word Bank Prepositions of time

at	four o'clock/night
in	the morning/afternoon/evening
on	Monday/Tuesday
from	half past three **to** quarter past four
after	school/quarter past three
before	lunch/half past six

▶ Language File page 117

6 PRONUNCIATION

🔘 2.08 Listen and write these words in the correct column.

evening history languages physical
Saturday subject timetable Wednesday

■ ■	■ ■ ■
evening	*languages*

Now listen and check. Repeat the words.

7 WRITING

Interview another student and note down the answers.

When do you …
get up in the morning?
have breakfast?
go to school?
come home?
have dinner?
go to bed?

Now write a paragraph describing the student's day.

Nicole gets up at quarter past seven in the morning.

Compare your paragraph with other students' paragraphs.

Extension Write a paragraph describing your day.

LANGUAGE WORKOUT

Complete.

Present simple
Questions
Do you/they like …?
_____ he/she/it like …?

Short answers
Yes, I/we/they _____.
No, I/we/they don't.
Yes, he/she/it does.
No, he/she/it _____.

▶**Answers and Practice**
Language File pages 116–117

3

3 I never lift weights

Saying how often you do things
Adverbs of frequency

1 OPENER

Where are Katya and Emily? Which of these can you see?

> **Word Bank** Sport and the gym
>
> exercise bike rowing machine
> running machine swimming pool
> tennis court weights

2 READING

2.09 Read the dialogue. Do both girls go to the gym every week?

KATYA This is a fantastic gym! How often do you come here?

EMILY I usually come on Monday after school. The training session for teenagers is from four to five o'clock every day. And I sometimes come at weekends.

KATYA Do you always start on the running machine?

EMILY Yes, I do. Then I get on the exercise bike. But I never lift weights.

KATYA Why not?

EMILY Weights are for over-16-year-olds – I'm only 14. What about you? Do you go to a gym?

KATYA Yes, we have a really good gym near our flat. I often go there in the morning before school – it's always busy in the afternoon.

EMILY And what do you do?

KATYA It depends, but I usually start on the rowing machine. And I always go to the dance classes on Wednesday.

EMILY What kind of dance classes?

KATYA We learn different dance routines like hip-hop and jive.

EMILY That sounds great!

3 AFTER READING

Correct the sentences.

1 Emily usually comes to the gym on Monday before school.
2 Emily sometimes starts on the running machine.
3 Emily often lifts weights.
4 Katya often goes to the gym after school.
5 The gym near Katya's flat is never busy in the afternoon.
6 Katya sometimes starts on the rowing machine.
7 Katya often goes to dance classes on Wednesday.

Your response Do you go to the gym?
What do you do there?

4 LISTENING

Look at the chart and match the pictures with these phrases.

> **Word Bank** Leisure activities and sport
>
> go dancing   go running   go shopping
> go swimming   go to the cinema   play basketball
> play football   play tennis   play volleyball

2.10 Now listen and note down how often Pierre and Emily do things.

	Pierre	How often?	Emily	How often?
Monday	🏊	*always*	🏃	
Tuesday	🏀		🏊	
Wednesday	⚽		🛍️	
Thursday	🏃		🎾	
Friday	🎬		💃	
Saturday	🏐		🎬	
Sunday	🏊		🛍️	

Talk about Pierre and Emily.

> Pierre always goes swimming on Monday.

Now talk about your week.

> I often go to the cinema on Friday.

Extension Write six sentences about your week.

5 PRONUNCIATION

2.11 Listen and repeat.

> /ŋ/
> dancing   evening   morning   ring
> rowing   running   shopping
> something   song   swimming   wrong

6 SPEAKING

Interview three students and complete the chart with A (*always*), U (*usually*), O (*often*), S (*sometimes*) or N (*never*).

> Do you go to bed late at the weekend?

> I usually go to bed late on Saturday. But I always go to bed early on Sunday.

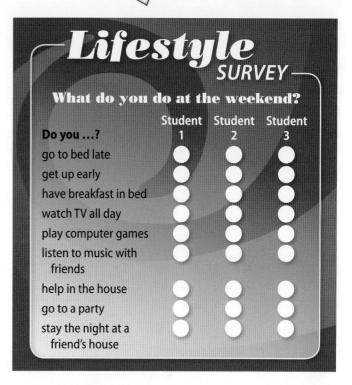

Lifestyle SURVEY

What do you do at the weekend?

Do you ...?	Student 1	Student 2	Student 3
go to bed late	○	○	○
get up early	○	○	○
have breakfast in bed	○	○	○
watch TV all day	○	○	○
play computer games	○	○	○
listen to music with friends	○	○	○
help in the house	○	○	○
go to a party	○	○	○
stay the night at a friend's house	○	○	○

Extension Compare two of the students.

> Anna always gets up early at the weekend but Paul never does.

7 WRITING

Write an email to a friend about your weekend, using your answers to the questions in the Lifestyle Survey.

At the weekend I often …

> **LANGUAGE WORKOUT**
>
> Complete with *after/before*.
>
> **Adverbs of frequency**
> always   usually   often   sometimes   never
>
> It is always busy.   Pronoun + *be* + adverb
> I often go there.   Pronoun + adverb + verb
>
> The adverb goes _____ the verb *be*.
> The adverb goes _____ other verbs.
>
> ►**Answers and Practice**
> Language File page 117

Personal profiles

Let's meet ...
Lewis Hamilton!

Lewis Hamilton, born 7th January 1985, is a motor racing star from Britain. He has short black hair and brown eyes, and he is very popular. Lewis has a house in Switzerland, but he races all over the world.

Between races, Lewis usually goes to the gym and works hard on his physical and mental fitness. He goes running in the morning before most people have breakfast. At race weekends he has a regular routine: he gets up early, he works with his team on his car, and he goes to bed at the same time every evening.

Lewis loves Japanese food and all kinds of spicy food. What else does he like? He plays pool with his brother Nic and goes ten-pin bowling with his mother. He also enjoys golf and swimming. Music? He likes hip-hop, R&B and reggae, and he loves jazz and blues. His favourite rapper is P Diddy. He enjoys movies. But it isn't easy to go to the movies when there are lots of newspaper photographers outside the cinema!

In the summer, Lewis usually goes to his family's holiday home in Portugal and he sometimes has Mediterranean boat holidays.

1 OPENER

Look at the photo. Which of these words do you expect to find in the magazine article?

> boat car fitness gym holiday
> maths race routine star volleyball

2 READING

🔘 **2.12** Read *Let's meet … Lewis Hamilton!* and answer the questions.

1 How old is Lewis Hamilton?
2 Where is he from?
3 What does he look like?
4 When does he get up at race weekends?
5 What sports and games does he enjoy?
6 What kind of music does he like?
7 Does he like movies?
8 Where does he usually go on holiday?

3 LISTENING

🔘 2.13 Read this email from Emily to her new epal. There are six mistakes in the email. Then listen to Emily and correct the mistakes.

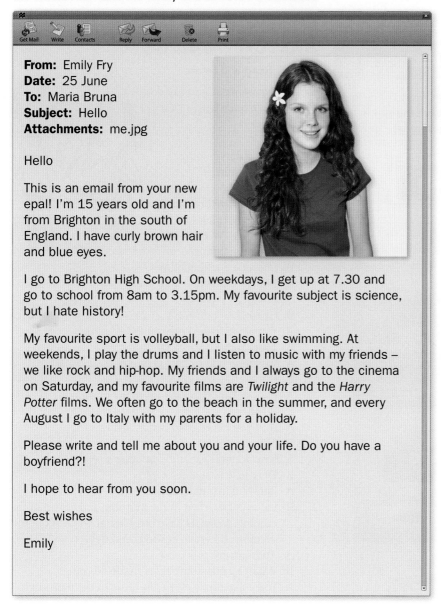

From: Emily Fry
Date: 25 June
To: Maria Bruna
Subject: Hello
Attachments: me.jpg

Hello

This is an email from your new epal! I'm 15 years old and I'm from Brighton in the south of England. I have curly brown hair and blue eyes.

I go to Brighton High School. On weekdays, I get up at 7.30 and go to school from 8am to 3.15pm. My favourite subject is science, but I hate history!

My favourite sport is volleyball, but I also like swimming. At weekends, I play the drums and I listen to music with my friends – we like rock and hip-hop. My friends and I always go to the cinema on Saturday, and my favourite films are *Twilight* and the *Harry Potter* films. We often go to the beach in the summer, and every August I go to Italy with my parents for a holiday.

Please write and tell me about you and your life. Do you have a boyfriend?!

I hope to hear from you soon.

Best wishes

Emily

4 SPEAKING

Complete these questions with *How, What, When* and *Where*.

1 _____ old are you?
2 _____ are you from?
3 _____ do you look like?
4 _____ do you get up on weekdays?
5 _____'s your favourite school subject?
6 _____ are your favourite sports?
7 _____ kind of music do you like?
8 _____ films do you like?
9 _____ do you go for your summer holiday?

Now ask another student the questions.

5 WRITING

Write an email to a new epal about you and your life. Use Emily's email to help you.

LEARNER INDEPENDENCE

6 Classroom English: Match the questions with the answers.

1 What's the English word for … ?

2 What's this called?

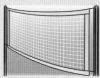

3 How do you say … in English?

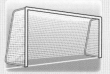

4 What's … in English?

Answers
skate   goal   net   racket

7 Add these sections to your vocabulary notebook. Write at least five words in each section.

Food   Sport and the gym
Leisure activities
School subjects

8 🔘 2.14 **Phrasebook:** Find these useful expressions in Unit 3. Then listen and repeat.

> Go away!
> Stop it!
> How often do you come here?
> Why not?
> What about you?
> It depends.
> That sounds great!

Now write a three-line dialogue using one or more of the expressions.

A *I love chocolate. What about you?*
B *I don't really like it.*
A *Why not?*

Inspiration EXTRA!

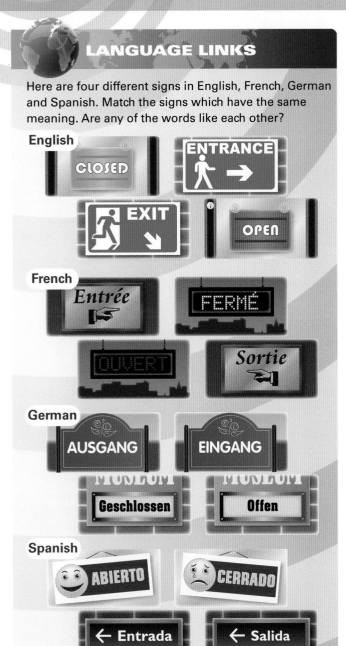

LANGUAGE LINKS

Here are four different signs in English, French, German and Spanish. Match the signs which have the same meaning. Are any of the words like each other?

English

CLOSED

ENTRANCE

EXIT

OPEN

French

Entrée

FERMÉ

OUVERT

Sortie

German

AUSGANG

EINGANG

Geschlossen

Offen

Spanish

ABIERTO

CERRADO

Entrada

Salida

SKETCH *The Survey*

🔘 2.15 Read and listen.

A Excuse me. Can I ask you some questions – for a survey?

B OK.

A When do you have breakfast in the morning?

B I never have breakfast in the morning.

A Oh, I see. What do you eat at lunchtime?

B I never eat at lunchtime.

A Really? When do you usually have dinner in the evening?

B Guess!

A You never have dinner in the evening.

B That's right.

A When do you usually get up in the morning?

B I …

A I know! You never get up in the morning!

B Right.

A And you never go to bed at night.

B Never.

A So you never eat and you never sleep.

B Of course I eat and sleep!

A But – I don't understand.

B I always go to bed in the morning and get up in the evening. I usually have breakfast at about six in the evening and lunch at about midnight.

A And dinner?

B When I come home at six in the morning.

A You come home every day at six in the morning?

B Yes – I work all night and sleep all day. Now it's six pm and it's time for breakfast. Excuse me!

Now act out the sketch in pairs.

Game *Word Race*

Work in pairs and name:

1 One kind of food that is yellow.

2 Two words for meals.

3 Two things you can do at the gym.

4 Three sports ending in -*ball*.

5 Three days of the week with six letters.

6 Three words ending with the sound /ŋ/.

7 Four prepositions of time.

8 Four months of the year ending with the letter *y*.

9 Four leisure activities.

10 Four kinds of food beginning with the letter *c*.

11 Five colours.

12 Five school subjects.

13 Five numbers beginning with the letter *f*.

14 Five letters which rhyme with *B*.

15 Five names of kinds of clothes.

REVISION

LESSON 1 Write three sentences about food you like and don't like.

I like ... but I don't like ... .

LESSON 2 Write questions and then answer them.

I get up at six in the morning.
Do you get up at six in the morning? No, I don't.

I walk to school every day.
We have a short break in the morning.
I do drama after school.
We have maths on Monday.
I go to bed at ten o'clock.

LESSON 3 Look at the chart in exercise 4 on page 43. Write three sentences about Pierre and three sentences about Emily.

Pierre always goes swimming on Monday.

LESSON 4 Look at the corrected email in exercise 3 on page 45. Write Emily's answers to the questions in exercise 4.

I'm from Brighton.

EXTENSION

LESSON 1 Use a bilingual dictionary and add ten new food words to your vocabulary notebook. Then write sentences saying which ones you like and don't like.

LESSON 2 Write six sentences about your school timetable. Write what subjects you study, on which day and at what time.

I do science on Friday at 10.05.

LESSON 3 Write sentences about things you don't often/usually do.

I don't often go to the gym.
I don't usually ...

LESSON 4 Look at *Let's meet ... Lewis Hamilton!* on page 44 and write a profile of the student you interviewed in exercise 4.

YOUR CHOICE!

SPORTS STAR POSTER

- Write about a sports star. Think about:
  His/Her training routine
  Favourite food and music
  Food, leisure activities and holidays
- Draw pictures or find photographs from magazines or the Internet for your poster.
- Show your Sports Star poster to other students.

FOOD MEMORY CHAIN

- Work in a small group.
- Student A says, for example:
  I like cheese.
- Student B repeats the sentence and adds to it.
  I like cheese and apples.
- Student C repeats Student B's sentence and adds to it.
  I like cheese and apples and tomatoes.
- The student with the best memory is the winner.

3 Culture

Take two teenagers ... north and south

1 OPENER

The texts in this lesson are about teenagers in Argentina and Estonia. Which country is in the north, and which is in the south?

READING

2 🔘 2.16 Read the texts about Piret and Emiliano. Match these topics with paragraphs 1–4 in each text.

School   Leisure activities
Family   Food

3 Answer the questions.

Who ...
1 lives in Argentina?
2 has one brother?
3 gets up at half past six?
4 walks to school?
5 starts school at quarter to eight?
6 goes to school for six hours a day?
7 studies Spanish?
8 likes school?
9 wears a school uniform?
10 likes pizza?
11 goes rollerblading?
12 plays the guitar?

FINLAND
Gulf of Finland
Tallinn
BALTIC SEA
ESTONIA
RUSSIA
LATVIA

Piret

1 'I live in Tallinn in the north-west of Estonia. I'm 15 and I live with my parents and brother in a small flat.

2 On weekdays, I get up at 7.00 in the morning. I usually wear jeans with a sweatshirt or pullover, and trainers. I walk to school – it's very near my home and we don't have a car. School starts at 8am and ends at 2pm. We have seven 45-minute lessons a day with 10-minute breaks. I study maths, biology, history, art, music, English and German – and Estonian, of course. My favourite subjects are English and history. I like school, and I have lots of friends there.

3 After school I go home for lunch. We usually have soup, and we often have potatoes and meatballs. They're my favourite food. I do my homework in the evening and I usually go to bed at 11pm.

4 In my free time, I go to the movies, visit friends and go rollerblading. I play tennis in the summer and go skiing in the winter. Our summer holiday is in July and August and we go to the Baltic Sea.'

VOCABULARY

4 Complete the words on the compass. You can find all the words in this lesson.

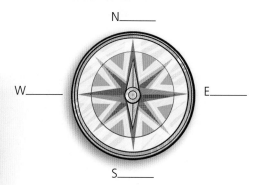

N_____

W_____   E_____

S_____

5 Look at the texts again and find:

- four words for sport
- six words for clothes
- seven words for food
- eight words for school subjects

6 SPEAKING

Compare the two teenagers' lives.

Same

> They both live in flats.

Different

> Piret lives in a small flat, but Emiliano lives in a big flat.

7 MINI-PROJECT
Lifestyle

Compare your life with either Piret's or Emiliano's life. Use the text to help you.

Piret lives in Tallinn in Estonia, but I live in ...

PARAGUAY

BRAZIL

PACIFIC OCEAN

URUGUAY

Buenos Aires

ARGENTINA

CHILE

ATLANTIC OCEAN

Emiliano

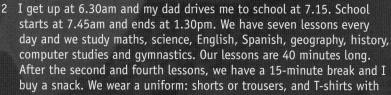

1 'I'm 14 and I live in Buenos Aires, in the east of Argentina. We have a big flat, but we're a big family – I have two brothers and three sisters.

2 I get up at 6.30am and my dad drives me to school at 7.15. School starts at 7.45am and ends at 1.30pm. We have seven lessons every day and we study maths, science, English, Spanish, geography, history, computer studies and gymnastics. Our lessons are 40 minutes long. After the second and fourth lessons, we have a 15-minute break and I buy a snack. We wear a uniform: shorts or trousers, and T-shirts with the school's name on.

3 I have lunch at home at 2pm with my brothers and sisters. We usually have meat and salad, and then fruit. But my favourite food is pizza. After lunch, I do my homework and in the evening I usually watch TV. I go to bed late, at half past eleven.

4 I play computer games or listen to music in my free time. My favourite music is rock and I play the guitar. At the weekend, I play football – everyone in Argentina likes football! – and we often drive to the countryside. Our summer holiday is from January to February and we usually go to the beach at Mar del Plata, south of Buenos Aires.'

1

How many ghosts are there?

Describing places and facilities
there is/are

1 OPENER

Look at the photos in the sightseeing guide. Which of these words do you expect to find in the text?

aquarium attractions beach ghosts history maths
museum pier sea sharks timetable tourists

2 READING

2.17 Read the sightseeing guide and match the attractions with the photos.

BRIGHTON
– city by the sea

Brighton is on the south-east coast of England, about 90km from London. Come and visit this exciting city – it has something for everyone.

There are lots of attractions for teenagers, including the **Brighton Museum & Art Gallery**, with information about the city and its history, and the **Sea Life Centre**, a fantastic aquarium with sharks and an underwater tunnel. You can go to the beach for all kinds of **water sports** and, of course, you can always have a swim – don't worry, there aren't any sharks in the sea! And in the evenings there's music and an open-air cinema on the beach.

Brighton is fantastic for shopping, and there are great shops, restaurants and cafés in **The Lanes**. And there are lots of ghosts in these old narrow streets. How many ghosts are there? Are there any scary ones? Go on a **ghost walk** and find out!

Can tourists see everything in Brighton in one day? No, there isn't time. But is there a place that everyone visits? Yes, there's a famous pier – the **Palace Pier**. It's 525 metres long, and at the end of the pier there's a funfair with exciting rides.

3 AFTER READING

Match the questions with the answers. There is one wrong answer.

1 Is Brighton on the south-east coast of England?
2 Is there an aquarium in Brighton?
3 Where can you go for water sports?
4 Are there any sharks in the sea?
5 Is there time to see everything in Brighton in one day?
6 Are there funfair rides on the pier?

a No, there aren't.
b To the beach.
c On a ghost walk.
d Yes, there are.
e Yes, there is.
f No, there isn't.
g Yes, it is.

Your response Do you want to visit Brighton? Why/Why not?

4 SPEAKING

Look at the sightseeing guide. What is there in the photos? How many?

bags   a beach   a bicycle   boats   a cat   chairs
cars   a cinema   ghosts   a museum   people
a restaurant   a school   shops   signs   umbrella

There's a beach.   There are lots of chairs.

Now say what there isn't in the photos.

There isn't a bicycle.   There aren't any ghosts.

Extension Play the *Memory game*: Student A closes the book. Student B asks questions about the photos.
A Is there a …? Are there any …?
B Yes, there is/are. OR No, there isn't/aren't.

5 PRONUNCIATION

2.18 Listen to the intonation and decide: Up ↗ or Down ↘?

1 There's a famous pier.
2 Are there any tourists?
3 Is there a restaurant?
4 There isn't a school.
5 How many shops are there?

Now listen again and repeat.

6 LISTENING

2.19 Mr Ward is telling the group about four Brighton attractions. Listen and complete with these names.

Jake   Katya   Pierre   Teresa

1 _____ thinks museums are boring.
2 _____ wants to go on a ghost walk.
3 _____ thinks sharks are scary.
4 _____ wants to go to Brighton Pier.

7 VOCABULARY

Ask and answer questions about your classroom. Think about size (*big/small*) and colour.

Word Bank Furniture and equipment
bags   blinds   books   boards   CD players
chairs   computers   desks   doors   lights
pictures   phones   televisions   windows

How many windows are there?   There are four big ones.

How many televisions are there?   There aren't any.

8 WRITING

Write a paragraph describing your classroom.

In my classroom there are four big windows.

Extension Choose things in your classroom and say how many there are. Can other students guess the missing words?

There are 30 …   … chairs!

LANGUAGE WORKOUT

Complete.

there is/ are
Affirmative
_____ is a famous pier.
There _____ lots of attractions.

Negative
There _____ time.
_____ aren't **any** sharks in the sea.

Questions
Is _____ a place that everyone visits?
How _____ ghosts _____ there?
Are _____ **any** scary ones?

▶**Answers and Practice**
Language File page 117

2 She's wearing a long grey coat

Describing what's happening now (1)
Present continuous: affirmative

1 OPENER

Look at the photo. What can you see?

2 READING

2.20 Read the dialogue. Why is Adam scared?

A guide is taking the group on a ghost walk.

GUIDE Now we're standing outside the theatre – it has a famous ghost called the Grey Lady …

ADAM Oh, this is silly. There aren't any ghosts here. It's raining and I'm going home.

TERESA Wait, look at that woman! Is she a ghost?

ADAM What! Where?

TERESA She's coming out of the theatre – she's wearing a long grey coat.

KATYA Her face is really white!

PIERRE Look! She's holding a red book.

TERESA And she's speaking …

ADAM Oh no! She's walking this way.

KATYA Adam, you're scared!

GUIDE But it isn't a ghost! It's an actor from the theatre. She's learning her lines!

3 AFTER READING

True or false? Correct the false sentences.

1 The ghost at the theatre is called the Black Lady.
2 The woman is wearing a grey coat.
3 She is holding a newspaper.
4 She is singing.
5 The woman in grey is an actor.

Your response Do you believe in ghosts?

4 GAME

Play *Guess what I'm holding!*

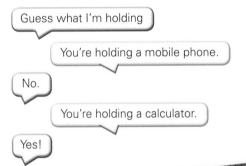

Guess what I'm holding

You're holding a mobile phone.

No.

You're holding a calculator.

Yes!

5 PRONUNCIATION

 2.21 Listen and repeat.

/ʌ/ come	/əʊ/ home
colour	coast
love	coat
mother	ghost
worry	hold

Now listen and write these words under *come* or *home*.

brother comb hope month
old one photo son

6 SPEAKING

Look at pictures A and B. Can you find ten differences?

Compare the pictures using these verbs.

draw hold look paint
play read sing stand wear

> In picture A, the woman is singing.

> In picture B, she's playing the piano.

7 WRITING

Look at the photo on pages 6–7 and write sentences describing the people.

Teresa is standing on the right. She's wearing a pink top, blue jeans and gold sandals.

Extension Read out your sentences but don't say the names. Can other students guess them?

LANGUAGE WORKOUT

Complete.

Present continuous: affirmative

Full forms	Contractions
I am speaking.	_____ speaking
You _____ speaking.	You're speaking.
He/She/It _____ speaking.	_____/She's/It's speaking.
We are speaking.	We're _____.
They _____ speaking.	They're speaking.

▶ **Answers and Practice**
Language File pages 117–118

What's she doing?

Describing what's happening now (2)
Present continuous: negative, questions and short answers

A

B

1 OPENER

Which of these can you see in the photos?

arms   books   feet   a football   hands   a helmet
a menu   a phone   shorts   a sign   a television

2 READING

 2.22   Read dialogues 1–3 and match them
with photos A–C.

The group are walking around Brighton.

1
EMILY   Look at the girl with a helmet on her head.
JAKE   Are you talking about the one in the
        pink top.
EMILY   Yes, what's she doing?
JAKE   She's going very fast – is she running?
EMILY   No, she isn't. She's rollerblading.

2
PIERRE Can you see the people with their
        arms in the air?
TERESA Yes, they're wearing white clothes.
        Are they dancing?
PIERRE No, they aren't. I think they're doing exercises.
TERESA Yes, they are. They're doing yoga.

3
ADAM   I can smell food!
KATYA   Let's get something to eat.
ADAM   See that sign? That man is selling fish and chips.
KATYA   Right. Is he selling ice cream too?
ADAM   I don't know, but I'm hungry!

C

3 AFTER READING

What are the people in photos A–C doing? Ask and
answer.

Your response
Do you like rollerblading?
Do you do exercises?
Are you hungry?

4 VOCABULARY

Look at the picture of the boy and match the words for parts of the body with numbers 1–16.

> **Word Bank** Parts of the body
>
> arm   ear   eye   face   finger   foot (*plural* feet)
> hair   hand   head   knee   leg   mouth
> nose   thumb   toe   tooth (*plural* teeth)

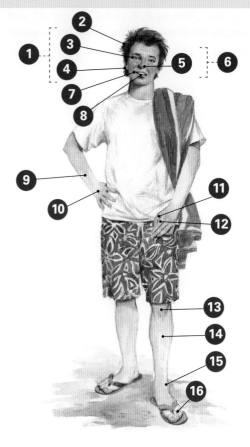

 Now listen and check.

5 SPEAKING

Point at the picture of the boy. Ask and answer.

> What am I pointing at?   His thumb.

> **Extension** Match parts of the body with these verbs.
>
> eat   hear   hold   point   run
> see   smell   think   walk
>
> *mouth/teeth – eat*

6 PRONUNCIATION

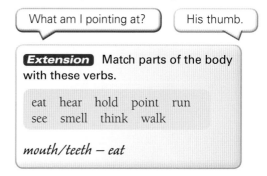 Listen and repeat.

> comb   ghost   guide   knee
> right   sign   talk   thumb   walk

Now cross out the silent letters.

comb

7 LISTENING

2.25 What are the people doing? Listen and choose.

1 Emily: sing a song/play the saxophone
2 Jake: use a computer/send a text message
3 Pierre and Adam: play tennis/play basketball
4 Katya: wash her hands/clean her teeth
5 Mr Ward: run/swim
6 Mr and Mrs Fry: have lunch/watch TV

Now ask and answer.

> Is Emily singing?

> What's Jake doing?

8 WRITING

Write sentences about the people in exercise 7.

Emily isn't singing. She's ...

> **Extension** Mime sports activities. Can other students guess what you are doing?
>
> Are you skateboarding?
>
> No, I'm not!

LANGUAGE WORKOUT

Complete.

Present continuous
Negative

Full forms	Contractions
I am not speaking.	I'm not speaking.
He/She/It _____ not speaking.	He/She/It isn't speaking.
We/You/They are not speaking.	We/You/They _____ speaking.

Questions	Short answers
Am I speaking?	Yes, you are.
	No, you _____.
_____ you speaking?	Yes, I am.
	No, _____ not.
	Yes, we _____.
	No, we aren't.
Is he/she/it speaking?	Yes, he/she/it _____.
	No, he/she/it isn't.
_____ they speaking?	Yes, they are.
	No, they aren't.

▶**Answers and Practice**
Language File pages 117–118

4 Integrated Skills
Describing places and activities

1 OPENER

Look at all the pictures in this lesson and find these things as quickly as possible.

> beds   a blind   books   a CD player
> chairs   a chest of drawers   curtains
> flowers   light   magazines   posters
> tables   a TV   a wardrobe   windows

2 READING

2.26 Read *The Treasures of Tutankhamun*. Then look at these sentences and decide: true, false or no information? Correct the false sentences.

1 Tutankhamun's treasures are in Egypt.
2 All the objects from Tutankhamun's tomb are gold.
3 In the museum you can see beds and chairs which are over 5,000 years old.
4 You can play games and musical instruments in the museum.
5 Lots of tourists go to see the treasures of Tutankhamun.

3 LISTENING

2.27 Look at pictures A, B and C on page 57 and listen to two phone conversations. Answer the questions.

Phone call 1
1 Who is Teresa talking to?
2 What is Teresa doing?
3 Which bedroom is she describing: A, B or C?

Phone call 2
5 Who is Pierre talking to?
6 What is Pierre doing?
7 Which bedroom is he describing: A, B or C?

The Treasures of Tutankhamun

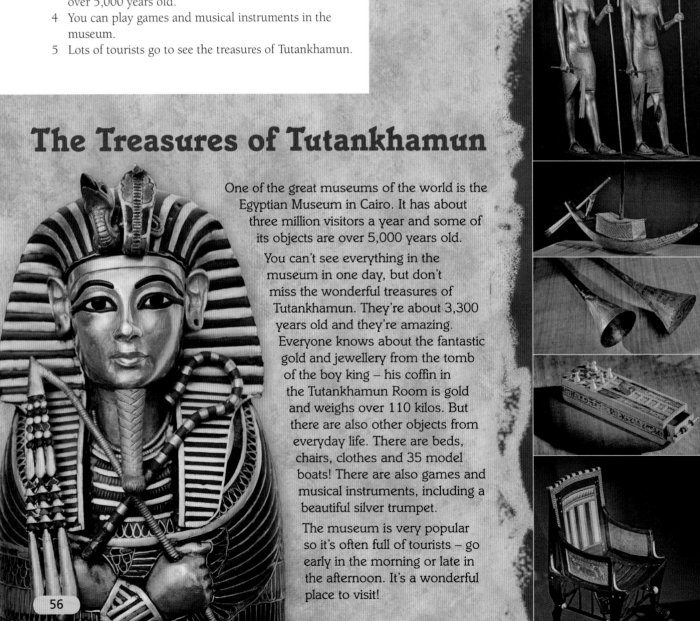

One of the great museums of the world is the Egyptian Museum in Cairo. It has about three million visitors a year and some of its objects are over 5,000 years old.

You can't see everything in the museum in one day, but don't miss the wonderful treasures of Tutankhamun. They're about 3,300 years old and they're amazing. Everyone knows about the fantastic gold and jewellery from the tomb of the boy king – his coffin in the Tutankhamun Room is gold and weighs over 110 kilos. But there are also other objects from everyday life. There are beds, chairs, clothes and 35 model boats! There are also games and musical instruments, including a beautiful silver trumpet.

The museum is very popular so it's often full of tourists – go early in the morning or late in the afternoon. It's a wonderful place to visit!

A

B

C

4 SPEAKING

Look at the picture of the room which Teresa and Pierre did not describe. Tell each other what you can see in the room.

Now take turns to describe one of the rooms and the other students guess: A, B or C.

5 WRITING

Write an email to an epal describing your room at home and what you are doing.

- Where are you sitting?
- What is there in your room?
- What are the other members of your family doing?

Hello!
I'm writing this in my room at home. I'm …

LEARNER INDEPENDENCE

6 Classroom English: Put these words in the right order to make sentences. You can use the sentences to ask your teacher or another student for help.

1 understand I sorry don't
2 right excuse this is me?
3 word say you this do how?
4 mean does what that?
5 again say that you can?
6 help please you me can?
7 doing exercise we which are?
8 please what answer is right the?

🔘 2.28 Now listen and check.

7 Add these sections to your vocabulary notebook.

Town facilities and attractions
Furniture
Parts of the body

8 🔘 2.29 Phrasebook: Find these useful expressions in Unit 4. Then listen and repeat.

No, there isn't time.
Oh, this is silly.
It's raining.
I'm going home.
Wait! Look! Oh no!
You're scared!
What's she doing?
I don't know.

Now write a three-line dialogue using one or more of the expressions.

A *Look! He's walking this way!*
B *Oh no! I'm going home.*
A *You're scared!*

Inspiration EXTRA!

PROJECT *Leisure activities*

Leisure activities in Brighton

Swimming, gym and other sports

The Prince Regent Swimming Complex is very near the Royal Pavilion. It has four swimming pools and a great gym. It's open from 7am to 10pm on weekdays, 9am to 6pm on Saturday and 9am to 10pm on Sunday.

Skateboarding

There are lots of parks in Brighton with great places to skate, and Brighton Youth Centre runs sessions for teenagers on Monday and Friday evenings at *'Da Roof'* *Indoor Skate-Park* in the centre of the city. All sessions cost £2.

1   Work in a group and look again at the text about Brighton in Unit 4 Lesson 1, and the Word Bank in Unit 3 Lesson 3. Make a list of leisure facilities in your town. Think about:

- **Taking part**
  playing indoor/outdoor games   water sports
  winter sports   dancing   fitness and gymnastics
  skateboarding, climbing, cycling, horse-riding, etc.

- **Watching/Listening**
  cinema   theatre   music   sport

2   Research: Choose two or three leisure activities to write about. Find out information about local facilities, for example:

- Where is it?
- What can you do there?
- When can you go there?
- How much does it cost?

3   Work together and write about the leisure facilities for a tourist information leaflet. Read your work carefully and correct any mistakes. Draw pictures or find photos from magazines or the Internet. Show your leaflet to the other groups.

Game   *Outside the room*

Form two teams: Red and Blue.

Red Team   A student goes outside the room and mimes an activity from the lists opposite.

Blue Team   A student stands by the open door. The Blue Team asks him/her *Yes/No* questions to guess the activity.

> Is she standing/sitting?

> Is she holding something? Is it a …? Is she …ing?

> Yes, she is./No, she isn't.

Then a student from the Blue Team goes outside …

Leisure activities	Home activities
Going to the movies	Making a phone call
Rollerblading	Having breakfast
Dancing	Cooking a meal
Skiing	Ironing a shirt
Playing an instrument	Doing homework
Swimming	Helping in the house
Lifting weights	Washing clothes
Playing computer games	Sewing on a button
Listening to music	Getting up
Watching TV	Going to bed

REVISION

LESSON 1 Write sentences about what there is in another student's bag or desk and your bag or desk.

There's a calculator in Hanna's bag but there isn't one in my bag.

LESSON 2 Look at the photo on page 14 and write sentences about what the people are doing and wearing.

Katya is pointing at the bicycles.

LESSON 3 Look at the photos on page 24. Write questions and answers about what people are doing/wearing.

What is Kumiko wearing?
She's wearing a black T-shirt.

LESSON 4 Look at the photos on page 57. Write a description of one of the rooms.

Room B. There are two windows ...

EXTENSION

LESSON 1 Write a description of what you can see from your classroom window.

LESSON 2 Write sentences about what other students in the classroom are doing.

Paul is looking out of the window.

LESSON 3 Choose four members of your family. Write sentences about what they are and aren't doing now.

My brother isn't doing his homework. He's watching TV.

LESSON 4 You are on holiday. Write a postcard to a friend describing your room and what you are doing.

I'm writing this in my room ...

YOUR CHOICE!

BACK TO BACK

- Work in pairs and stand back to back.
- Take turns to say what you think your partner is wearing. Don't look at each other!

  A You're wearing a green shirt ...
  B Yes, that's right.
  A ... and you're wearing black jeans.
  B No, I'm not. They're grey!

DESCRIBE AND DRAW A ROOM

- Work in a small group. You need a piece of paper and a pencil/pen.
- Work together to describe a room. Take turns to say what is in the room and where the items are. Draw the items in the right place. Don't look at each other's drawings!

  A There's a door on the left.
  B There's a table in the middle.
  C There are two chairs by the table.

- When your drawing is complete, compare it with the rest of the group

REVIEW

1 Read and complete. For each number 1–10, choose word A, B or C.

CYCLING THE WORLD

Mike Roots is from Colchester in the south-east of England. He is 67 years old and he is cycling round the world. But __1__ 13 years and 130,000 kilometres, he is still at home – __2__ an exercise bike. He rides the bike in his front room, and he __3__ maps to plan his route from country to country.

'My friends and family __4__ I am mad. I love cycling but I __5__ like the roads these days – they're really dangerous when you're on a bike,' says Mr Roots. 'I get guide books and maps, and I __6__ all about the countries on my route, so it's like a holiday.'

Mr Roots rides his exercise bike __7__ day and he __8__ down the number of kilometres he cycles. He tries to do 240 kilometres a week. At the moment he is __9__ up the coast of Argentina. '__10__ a long way to go through South and North America, Iceland, Greenland and then home.'

1 A before	B then	C after
2 A in	B on	C at
3 A use	B uses	C using
4 A think	B thinks	C thinking
5 A not	B doesn't	C don't
6 A learn	B learns	C learning
7 A always	B every	C usually
8 A write	B writes	C writing
9 A go	B goes	C going
10 A There's	B There are	C They're

2 Write sentences using the present simple.

1 Teresa/like/pizza
2 Adam/not have/a brother
3 they/hate/chocolate
4 Emily/not want/an ice cream
5 I/not speak/Italian
6 Ruby/not like/bananas
7 you/not want/eggs
8 we/love/fish

3 Complete the questions and answer them.

1 _____ Ruby like Pierre?
2 When _____ you come home from school?
3 What time _____ they have lunch at Brighton High School?
4 _____ Emily lift weights?
5 When _____ Katya go to dance classes?
6 What _____ Pierre always do on Monday?
7 _____ Emily play basketball on Thursday?
8 How often _____ you go to the cinema?

4 Write questions and short answers.

Pierre/play volleyball ✓
Does Pierre play volleyball? Yes, he does.
Katya/play volleyball ✗
Does Katya play volleyball? No, she doesn't.

1 Teresa/play football ✓
2 Pierre/like octopus ✗
3 Adam and Ruby/live in a cottage ✓
4 Katya/come from Switzerland ✗
5 Jake/love sport ✓
6 Ruby/play tennis ✗
7 Adam and Ruby/live in Geneva ✗
8 Adam/have geography on Thursday ✓

5 Complete with *at*, *in*, *on*, *from* or *to*.

1 I get up _____ seven o'clock _____ the morning.
2 They go to school _____ Monday _____ Friday.
3 Adam has maths _____ Friday.
4 You can't play football _____ night.
5 She comes home from school _____ four o'clock _____ the afternoon.
6 We have English _____ nine _____ ten on Tuesday.
7 They don't have school _____ the weekend.

6 Write sentences using the adverbs of frequency in *italics*.

1 Jake/go to the cinema/on Saturday   *often*
2 I/watch TV/in the morning   *never*
3 Emily/go running/on Monday   *usually*
4 we/be busy/at the weekend   *always*
5 they/go shopping/after school   *sometimes*

7 Write questions and answers about Teresa's bedroom in Valencia.

computer ✓
Is there a computer? Yes, there is.

1 posters ✓
2 desk ✗
3 curtains ✓
4 TV ✗
5 books ✓
6 wardrobe ✗
7 alarm clock ✓
8 flowers ✗

8 Write sentences using the present continuous.

1 Ruby/hold/a mobile phone
2 Adam and Jake/play/basketball
3 Mr Ward/stand/on the left
4 we/watch/TV
5 they/cook/Chinese food
6 Teresa/talk/to Pierre
7 the actor/learn her lines
8 I/have/breakfast

9 Write questions and answer them.

Emily is reading a magazine./Teresa ✓
Is Teresa reading a magazine? Yes, she is.

1 Katya is wearing a blue top./Teresa ✓
2 Emily and Pierre are playing tennis./Jake and Adam ✓
3 Jake and Pierre are eating ice creams./Katya and Teresa ✗
4 The guide is talking to the group./Mr Ward ✗
5 Pierre is staying with Adam./Jake ✗
6 Teresa is writing an email./Katya ✓
7 The girls are playing football./the boys ✓
8 Adam is playing the guitar./Jake ✗

10 Complete with the verbs in the present continuous.

On the ghost walk

JAKE   It's very dark and I can't see. What __1__ (happen)?
EMILY   Not a lot! We __2__ (wait) for Adam.
JAKE   Why __3__ (we/wait) for him?
EMILY   I think he __4__ (make) a phone call.
JAKE   No, he __5__ (not make) a phone call. I can see now. He __6__ (talk) to Teresa.
EMILY   What __7__ (they/talk) about?
JAKE   I don't know. I can't hear. They __8__ (laugh) about something.
EMILY   Oh, look! They __9__ (leave)!
JAKE   Hey, you two, where __10__ (you/go)?
TERESA Adam is scared. We __11__ (go) home.
JAKE   I don't think Adam is scared!
EMILY   Look! They __12__ (run) away.

VOCABULARY

11 Complete with ten of these words.

> beach break chair cottage flat
> hands late money restaurant smell
> sports subjects

1 Adam doesn't live in a house. He lives in a _____.
2 Pierre lives in a _____.
3 Teresa's school has a short _____ in the morning.
4 Volleyball and basketball are _____.
5 I often go to bed _____ on Friday.
6 History, maths and science are school _____.
7 You can swim in the sea or relax on the _____.
8 You hold something with your _____.
9 You can have a meal in a _____.
10 He's cooking a meal. I can _____ food.

12 Match these words with their definitions.

> breakfast egg exciting gym
> lunch museum theatre timetable
> umbrella weekend

1 The first meal of the day.
2 A place where there are exercise machines.
3 A place where actors work.
4 Saturday and Sunday.
5 It tells you the times of lessons.
6 A meal you eat in the middle of the day.
7 It comes from a chicken.
8 A place where you can learn about history.
9 You can use it when it is raining.
10 Opposite of *boring*.

13 Match the verbs in list A with the words and phrases in list B.

	A	B
1	go	a city
2	lift	a game
3	listen	a uniform
4	pay	food
5	play	for something
6	smell	to bed
7	visit	to music
8	wear	weights

LEARNER INDEPENDENCE
SELF ASSESSMENT

Look back at Lessons 1–3 in Units 3 and 4.

How good are you at …?	✓Fine	? Not sure
1 Talking about likes and dislikes Workbook p30 exercise 1	☐	☐
2 Talking about regular activities Workbook pp32–33 exercises 1, 3 and 6	☐	☐
3 Saying how often you do things Workbook pp34–35 exercises 1–5	☐	☐
4 Describing places and facilities Workbook pp42–43 exercises 1–3	☐	☐
5 Describing what's happening now Workbook pp44–45 exercises 1–4 and pp46–47 exercises 1–4	☐	☐

Not sure? Have a look at Language File pages 116–118 and do the Workbook exercise(s) again.

Now write an example for 1–5

1 I really don't like octopus.

61

PREVIEW

COMMUNICATIVE AIMS
LEARNING HOW TO ...

1 Talk about regular activities
2 Talk about what people are doing now
3 Talk about possessions
4 Make comparisons
5 Talk about past events
6 Ask about past events

TOPICS AND VOCABULARY

Routines
Jobs
Possessions
Weather
Seasons
Social situations
Town facilities
Continents and countries
Transport
Feelings

1 Match the pictures (A–F) with six items in the Topics and Vocabulary box.

2 Put the words into categories.

Jobs   Weather   Transport

waiter temperature hairdresser nurse taxi plane bus car model rainy sunny pilot windy train cloudy

She was in the park.

Whose is the blue bag?

I was quite cross.

3 Match the words with the pictures.

bread   castle   dolphin   firefighter   moon   trumpet

TODAY'S WEATHER

Amsterdam	☁ ☀ 🏴	17
Brighton	☁☁ 🏴	15°
London	☁☁🌧 🏴	
	☀	

It's rainier in London than in Mexico City.

My mother teaches maths and French.

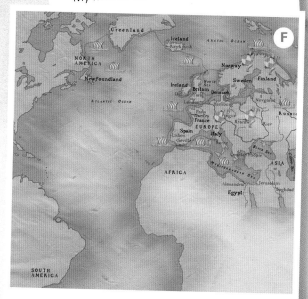

Some Vikings went east through Europe to Asia.

5 Do the Capital City Quiz with two other students.

CAPITAL CITY QUIZ

TRUE OR FALSE?

1 Mexico City is bigger than Geneva.

2 Madrid is higher than Amsterdam.

3 Rio de Janeiro is hotter than Moscow.

4 Rome is older than New York.

5 London is wetter than Cairo.

Answers to Quiz: All the facts are true.

4 🔘 2.30 Listen to extracts 1–3 from Units 5 and 6. Match them with these topics.

A   Social situations
B   Routines
C   Weather

Believe it or not!

Every year there are 16 million thunderstorms in the world! That's 1,800 thunderstorms every hour, and 6,000 flashes of lightning every minute!

1 # I'm having a wonderful time

Talking about regular activities
Talking about what people are doing now
Present simple and present continuous

1 OPENER

Look at the photo. Guess: Which of these words are in the text?

boat dolphin geography museum ocean
radio restaurant sailing sea stars tennis

2 READING AND LISTENING

🔘 2.31 Emily's cousin Cathy is working on a boat this summer.
Listen and complete her email with the times.

Get Mail Write Contacts Reply Forward Delete Print

Hello from the middle of the Atlantic Ocean!

We're sailing from Spain to Barbados in the
Caribbean Sea and I'm having a wonderful time. I'm
writing this on my laptop. It's a beautiful day, the sun
is shining and dolphins are playing around the boat
at the moment!

What's a typical day like at sea? Well, I get up at
___1___ and we have breakfast at ___2___ – we have
coffee and toast. At ___3___ I go on watch for three
hours. At midday I start cooking lunch and we
have lunch at ___4___. In the afternoon, we read and
sunbathe. At ___5___ I write emails and at ___6___ we
make a video call to our base in Brighton. Then we
listen to the news on the radio. We have dinner
at ___7___, and I go on watch again at ___8___ – I sit
outside and look at the stars. And at ___9___ I go to
sleep!

Now it's time to make the video call.

Love
Cathy

3 AFTER READING AND LISTENING

True or false? Correct the false sentences.

1 Cathy is sailing to Spain.
2 The weather is sunny.
3 They have tea and toast for breakfast.
4 She starts cooking lunch at noon.
5 In the afternoon, she writes emails.
6 They make a video call before dinner.

Your response Is this your kind of holiday?
Do you think sailing is fun?

4 SPEAKING

Ask and answer questions about routines on the
boat.

What time does
Cathy get up?

At 7am.

Now ask and answer questions about what's
happening at different times.

It's 7am now.
What's Cathy doing?

She's getting up.

5 READING

🔘 2.32 Read and match the job descriptions with the photos.

TERESA My father plays the trumpet in a jazz band. There's a great music scene in Valencia.

PIERRE My mother teaches maths and French at the World International School in Geneva.

KATYA My mother translates English and German into Russian at international conferences in Moscow.

JAKE My father works for the Washington DC Police Department and he drives a police car.

EMILY Mum works at Brighton hospital. She looks after people who are ill or hurt. She often works at night.

ADAM Dad works for British Airways. He flies planes to South-east Asia – that's why he's often away from home.

Steven Campbell · Valentina Petrova · Manuel Navarro · Christine Dubois · Ray Turner · Sarah Fry

6 VOCABULARY

Ask and answer questions about the people in the photos. Choose from these jobs.

Word Bank Jobs

cleaner doctor electrician firefighter
hairdresser interpreter journalist model
musician nurse pilot police officer
shop assistant taxi-driver teacher waiter

> What does Steven Campbell do?   He's a …

Now read the text in exercise 5 again. What are the people doing in the photos?

1 Steven is flying to Brazil/Japan.
2 Valentina is speaking Russian/German.
3 Manuel is playing the saxophone/trumpet.
4 Christine is teaching maths/Spanish.
5 Ray is/isn't driving a police car.
6 Sarah is looking after a woman/man.

Extension Ask other students questions about their family.

> What do your parents do?   What's your mother doing now?

7 PRONUNCIATION

🔘 2.33 Listen and repeat.

/ə/
assistant doctor firefighter hairdresser
interpreter journalist model musician pilot
police officer taxi-driver teacher waiter

Now circle the /ə/ sound.

assistant

8 WRITING

Choose two famous people. Write about what they do, and say what you think they're doing at the moment. Show your notes to other students.

Kate Moss is a model and designer. She models and designs clothes. I think she's designing a new dress at the moment.

LANGUAGE WORKOUT

Complete.

Present simple
At midday I **start** cooking lunch.
In the afternoon, they _____ (read) and sunbathe.
She _____ (sit) outside and _____ (look) at the stars.
We use the present simple to talk about **regular activities**.

Present continuous
We**'re sailing** from Spain to Barbados.
She _____ _____ (have) a wonderful time.
Dolphins _____ _____ (play) around the boat at the moment.
We use the present continuous to talk about what is happening **now**.

▶**Answers and Practice**
Language File page 117–118

Whose turn is it?

Talking about possessions
Possessive pronouns
Possessive 's
Question: *Whose ...?*

1 OPENER

Which of these can you see in the photo?

> a bottle of water   a camera   a cap   a silver earring
> a games console   a magazine   a packet of crisps
> a remote   sunglasses   a sweatshirt   trainers

2 READING

🔘 2.34   Read the dialogue. What's the problem?

The group are playing a video game on a games console.

EMILY   Well done, Teresa!

TERESA   Thanks. Who wants to play next?

ADAM   Whose turn is it?

JAKE   I think it's mine.

EMILY   No, it isn't yours. It's Adam's turn.

JAKE   Sorry, but it isn't his. It really *is* mine.

ADAM   Hey, what's the problem? We have two remotes
so we can have two teams. We can all play at the
same time.

TERESA   Good idea, Adam. You play with me and Emily
can play with Jake.

JAKE   But I want to play with *you*.

TERESA   Don't get cross, Jake. It's only a game.

3 AFTER READING

Match the questions with the answers. There is one
wrong answer.

1   Who is playing on the games console?
2   Whose turn is it?
3   Does Emily think it's Adam's turn?
4   What is Adam's idea?
5   Does Jake want to play with Emily?
6   Who gets cross?

a   Yes, she does.
b   Jake does.
c   Jake thinks it's his.
d   No, Jake isn't.
e   No, he doesn't.
f   Teresa is.
g   They can all play at the same time.

Your response Do you like video games?

4 SPEAKING

Look carefully at the photo on page 66. Ask and answer questions about these things.

> black T-shirt   blue bag   crisps   blue top
> grey sweatshirt   pink top   red cap   black jeans
> silver earring   sunglasses   watch

Whose is the blue bag?   It's Emily's.

Whose are the sunglasses?   They're Adam's.

Extension Borrow things from other students. Then work with a partner. Hold up each object and ask *Whose is this?*

5 PRONUNCIATION

🔘 2.35 Listen and repeat. <u>Underline</u> the stressed words.

Is it Adam's watch?
No, it isn't his. It's Teresa's.

Now ask and answer questions about these things.

1 Teresa's cap
2 Adam's earring
3 Jake's sunglasses
4 Teresa and Adam's crisps
5 Emily's sweatshirt
6 Teresa's bag

Listen and check.

6 SPEAKING

Ask and answer questions about the photos 1–8.

Whose hair is it?   I think it's Emily's.

I'm not sure. I think it's Katya's hair.

🔘 2.36 Now listen and check.

Extension Cut up pictures of famous people. Then ask another student about them.

Whose is this jacket?   Whose feet are these?

7 WRITING

Pierre and Katya find two bags. Complete the dialogue with apostrophes.

PIERRE Is this Jakes bag?
KATYA I dont know. Lets see whats inside. Whose magazines are these?
PIERRE They arent Jakes. Theyre in Spanish. I think theyre Teresas.
KATYA Yes, thats Teresas bag. But what about the blue bag?
PIERRE I think its Emilys – Im sure she likes blue.

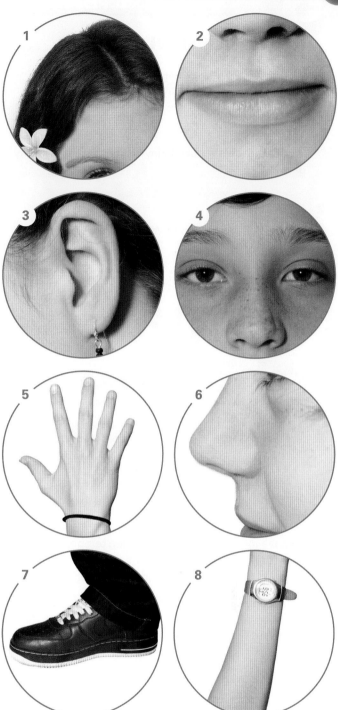

LANGUAGE WORKOUT

Complete.

Possessive adjectives	Possessive pronouns
my	_____
your	_____
his/her	_____/hers
our	ours
your	yours
their	theirs

Possessive 's
Adam**'s** turn

▶Answers and Practice
Language File page 118

It's sunnier

Making comparisons (1)
Comparative adjectives (-er, more)

1 OPENER

What's the weather like today? Is it hot or cold, sunny or rainy?

2 READING

◎ 2.37 Read *Climate change*. What information is surprising?

Climate change

Is the world's weather getting better or worse?

Well, we know that it's sunnier. World temperatures are 0.6°C higher than 100 years ago and central England is 1°C hotter than 30 years ago. And the seasons are changing. In Britain spring comes earlier, and autumn starts later and is longer.

Rain is a more difficult problem than temperature. We don't know how much it rains over the sea. But we know that it's now rainier in some parts of the world and drier in others. For example, the weather is wetter in winter in northern Europe and North America. In the tropics it's drier in summer than before.

What about the sea? Water expands and ice melts in warmer weather. The sea level varies in different parts of the world, but it's about 10–25cm higher than 100 years ago. Around Britain the sea is 10cm higher than in 1900. And scientists say that by 2100 many of the 1,192 islands of the Maldives in the Pacific Ocean are likely to be underwater.

Of course, over hundreds of years the Earth gets hotter and then it gets colder again. But scientists are sure that what's happening now is different. The world is getting warmer. For example, the way we use energy from coal and oil is making the planet hotter. This is one cause of climate change – and it's man-made.

3 AFTER READING

Choose the correct word.

1 Central England is hotter/colder than 30 years ago.
2 Spring in Britain is earlier/later.
3 Autumn in Britain is shorter/longer.
4 It's easier/more difficult to be sure about rain.
5 Winter is rainier/sunnier in the north.
6 Summer in the tropics is drier/wetter.
7 The sea is higher/hotter than 100 years ago.
8 Changes in temperature are new/old.

Your response What can we do about climate change?

4 VOCABULARY

Complete the words for the four seasons.

sp_____   su_____   a_____   w_____

Match these words with photos 1–6.

> **Word Bank** Weather
>
> cloudy   foggy   rainy   sunny   snowy   windy

Now compare the weather in different seasons.

> It's cloudier in spring than in summer.

5 SPEAKING

What about the weather in your country?

Think about these questions:

- Temperature: is it hotter in summer and colder in winter now?
- Rain: is it wetter or drier in the different seasons now?
- Seasons: are the times of the seasons changing?

> Is it hotter in summer now?

> Is it wetter in spring now?

Ask your teacher what he/she thinks.

> **Extension** Write sentences about changes in temperature, rain and the seasons in your country.

6 PRONUNCIATION

Circle the /ə/ sound in these words.

> /ə/
>
> autumn   Britain   drier   hotter   hundred   picture
> problem   season   summer   than   weather   wetter

🔘 2.38 Now listen and check. Repeat the words.

7 SPEAKING

Look at the chart and compare the weather.

TODAY'S WEATHER

Amsterdam	☁	☀	🌬	17°
Brighton	☁		🌬	15°
London	🌧		🌬	14°
Madrid		☀		30°
Mexico City	🌧	☀		27°
Moscow		☀		25°
New York	🌧		🌬	24°
Zurich	☁	☀		21°

> It's rainier in London than in Mexico City.

> It's hotter in Madrid than in Moscow.

> The weather in Brighton is worse than the weather in Zurich.

8 WRITING

Look at the chart in exercise 7 and write a paragraph comparing today's weather in your town/city and the cities in the chart.

Our weather is better/worse than London's.
It's hotter/colder in Madrid than here.

LANGUAGE WORKOUT

Complete.

Adjective	Comparative	Adjective	Comparative
cold	cold____	dry	dr**ier**
high	_____	easy	_____
short	_____	sunny	_____
late	late**r**		
		difficult	**more** difficult
big	bi**gger**	famous	_____ famous
hot	ho**tter**	expensive	_____ expensive
wet	wet____	popular	_____ popular

Irregular	
good	**better**
bad	**worse**

▶**Answers and Practice**
Language File pages 118–119

Questionnaire

Personality Test
What are

1 Which is your favourite colour?

A Red or yellow.
B Brown or grey.
C Blue or green.

2 When you are shopping, do you ...

A know what you want and buy it?
B ask for a friend's help?
C compare things in lots of shops?

4 Do you like it more when you are ...

A alone?
B with lots of people?
C with two or three friends?

3 When you are talking to someone, do you ...

A touch your hair or face?
B touch the person you are talking to?
C fold your arms?

5 When you see something funny, do you ...

A laugh a lot?
B laugh?
C smile?

7 Which is your favourite time of the day?

A The morning.
B The afternoon.
C Late at night.

6 Which is easier when you have a problem?

A To phone someone.
B To email someone.
C To go and see someone.

1 OPENER

Choose two of these adjectives to describe your personality.

Word Bank Personality adjectives

careful   confident   friendly   happy
helpful   open   quiet   serious   shy

2 READING

Read and answer the questionnaire. Then find out your score.

3 LISTENING

🔘 2.39 Listen and write down Emily's answers to the questionnaire. What is her score? What does it say about her personality?

you like?

8 **Which is your favourite evening activity?**

A Watching TV.
B Talking to a friend.
C Going to a party.

9 **How often do you wear the same clothes the next day?**

A Sometimes.
B Never.
C Very often.

10 **When you are angry with people, do you ...**

A shout at them?
B discuss the problem with them?
C say nothing?

Personality Test scores

1	A=6	B=2	C=4	**20–33 points**
2	A=6	B=4	C=2	You are quiet and careful. You are a serious person and think a lot
3	A=4	B=6	C=2	before you do something. You think a lot about other people too,
4	A=2	B=6	C=4	but are quite happy when you are alone.
5	A=6	B=4	C=2	**34–47 points**
6	A=4	B=2	C=6	You are a friendly, open, helpful person. Friends are important to
7	A=2	B=4	C=6	you and you always help them with their problems.
8	A=2	B=4	C=6	**48–60 points**
9	A=4	B=6	C=2	You are a confident person. You aren't at all shy and you enjoy life
10	A=6	B=4	C=2	a lot. You think quickly and often tell others what to do.

4 SPEAKING

Compare your score with other students' scores and Emily's score. What does your score say about your personality? Do you agree with your score? Is there anything you want to change in the description of your personality?

5 WRITING

Use your answers to the questionnaire and your score to write a paragraph about your personality.

My favourite colour is ...

LEARNER INDEPENDENCE

6 Classroom English: Match the words with the punctuation marks.

> **Word Bank** Punctuation
>
> brackets   capital letter   comma
> exclamation mark   full stop
> hyphen   question mark

2.40 Now listen and write the punctuation marks you hear.

7 Add these sections to your vocabulary notebook.

Jobs   Weather and seasons
Personality adjectives

8 **2.41** **Phrasebook:** Find these useful expressions in Unit 5. Then listen and repeat.

> I'm having a wonderful time.
> It's a beautiful day.
> It's time to …
> Well done!
> Whose turn is it?
> What's the problem?
> Good idea.

Now write a three-line dialogue using one or more of the expressions.

A *It's time to go home.*
B *Not now. I'm having a wonderful time.*
A *But it's three o'clock in the morning!*

Inspiration EXTRA!

LANGUAGE LINKS

Many words in English are like words in other languages. Which of these words are like words in your language?

International words in English
banana camera chocolate cinema club
drama football golf guitar jeans music
photograph pizza sandwich stop television
tennis video volleyball weekend

Find other words in Units 1–5 which are like words in your language. Make a section in your vocabulary notebook for these words. Notice the differences in spelling!

SKETCH *The Car*

2.42 Read and listen.

MAN	Excuse me. This car – is it yours?
WOMAN	Why?
MAN	It's outside my house. I don't want it here.
WOMAN	Why not?
MAN	I want to have *my* car outside my house. Can you please drive the car away?
WOMAN	No, I'm sorry, I can't.
MAN	You can't?
WOMAN	No.
MAN	I don't understand. Can't you drive?
WOMAN	Of course I can drive.
MAN	Then why can't you drive the car away?
WOMAN	I don't have the car keys.
MAN	You don't have the keys? But it's your car.
WOMAN	No, it isn't mine.
MAN	It isn't yours? Then whose is it?
WOMAN	I don't know. Oh, here's my bus. Bye!

Now act out the sketch in pairs.

Game What's My Job?

- Form two teams: Red and Blue.

- A Red Team student thinks of a job and mimes it for his/her team to guess. They ask questions using the present continuous and present simple.

- Then a Blue Team student thinks of a job and mimes it for his/her team to guess.

- Teams score a point for every job they guess in 60 seconds.

Q Are you driving a car?
A No, I'm not.
Q Do you travel a lot?
A Yes, I do.
Q Do you wear a uniform?
A Yes, I do.
Q Are you a train-driver?
A No, I'm not.
Q Do you go to lots of countries?
A Yes, I do.
Q Are you flying a plane?
A Yes, I am!
Q Are you a pilot?
A Yes, I am!

REVISION

LESSON 1 Look at Cathy's email on page 64. Write a description of her typical day at sea.

Cathy gets up at 7am and she has breakfast at 7.15.

LESSON 2 Look at the photo on page 66. Make a list of all the clothes and other things that the people are wearing and holding.

grey sweatshirt, blue bag, ...

LESSON 3 Look at the weather chart on page 69. Write sentences about today's weather in the cities.

In Brighton it's very cloudy and it's windy. The temperature is 15 degrees.

LESSON 4 Look at Emily's answers to the questionnaire on pages 70–71. Write a paragraph about her.

Emily's favourite time of the day is ...

EXTENSION

LESSON 1 Choose four members of your family. Write sentences about what they do, and say what they're doing at the moment.

My mother is a teacher. She's having lunch at the moment.

LESSON 2 Look at the photo on page 66. Write questions and answers about people's things.

Whose is the red cap?
It's Emily's.

LESSON 3 Make true sentences using these comparative adjectives.

> bigger   more expensive   more famous
> higher   more popular   smaller

Your shoes are bigger than mine.

LESSON 4 Write a paragraph about your best friend's personality. Use the questionnaire on pages 70–71 to help you.

YOUR CHOICE!

THINK OF A WORD!

- Work in pairs.
- Student A says a word for an object, for example, *wallet, photo, comb, guitar, camera, watch.*
- Student B says a word for each of these six categories:

  something smaller
  something bigger
  something earlier in the dictionary
  something later in the dictionary
  a shorter word
  a longer word

  A Wallet.
  B Earring, car, spring, windy, tea, sunglasses

WORLD WEATHER REPORT

- Work in a small group and find out information about weather in different parts of the world from newspapers or the Internet.
- Choose two places to write about and note down important information. For example:

  What's the temperature in January and in July?
  How much rain is there every year?
  Is it often windy?
  Does it snow in winter?

- Use your notes to write a *World Weather Report.* Show your report to other students.

SOCIAL SITUATIONS QUESTIONNAIRE

WHAT DOES IT MEAN?

There are more than 700,000 different gestures in the world! And some gestures mean different things in different places! What do these gestures mean in your country?

1

A Help!
B I have no idea.
C I don't have any money.
D *Another meaning?*

2

A Goodbye.
B Listen to me.
C Come here.
D *Another meaning?*

3

A We're very good friends.
B Let's hope for good luck.
C I'm not sure.
D *Another meaning?*

4

A Be quiet.
B One.
C Go away!
D *Another meaning?*

5

A That's great.
B One.
C Give me some money.
D *Another meaning?*

6

A Don't forget.
B He's crazy!
C I'm not sure.
D *Another meaning?*

1 READING

Read and answer the questionnaire.

2 LISTENING

2.43 Listen to Adam and Emily answering the questionnaire. What do the gestures mean in Britain? Are there any differences between Britain and your country?

3 READING

Read *What do you say at a party?* and choose the best responses.

2.44 Now listen and check.

4 SPEAKING

What do you say in these situations? Choose from the expressions below.

What do you say …

1 when someone sneezes?
2 when you want to talk to someone?
3 when you stand on someone's foot?
4 when you can't understand someone?
5 when someone doesn't look happy?
6 before someone goes on holiday?

a What's wrong?
b Can I have a word with you?
c Bless you!
d Have a fabulous time!
e Sorry? Can you say that again?
f I'm very sorry!

2.45 Now listen and check.

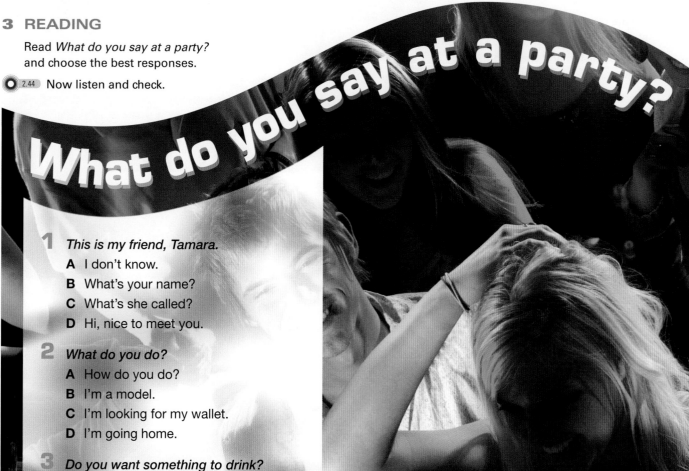

What do you say at a party?

1 *This is my friend, Tamara.*
 A I don't know.
 B What's your name?
 C What's she called?
 D Hi, nice to meet you.

2 *What do you do?*
 A How do you do?
 B I'm a model.
 C I'm looking for my wallet.
 D I'm going home.

3 *Do you want something to drink?*
 A Thank you.
 B Yes, please.
 C Yes, thank you.
 D Yes, I want.

4 *What's he like?*
 A He likes football and swimming.
 B He has brown hair and blue eyes.
 C He's feeling ill.
 D He's a great guy.

5 *Can I use your phone?*
 A Never mind.
 B Sorry, I can't.
 C Yes, of course.
 D I can't remember.

5 MINI-PROJECT
Gesture Guide

Work with another student and write a short guide to gestures in your country.

- Find four pictures of people making gestures. Look in newspapers and magazines or on the Internet. For example, look for gestures people make when they say goodbye, when they meet someone, or when they mean *Yes* or *No*.
- By each picture write the meaning of the gesture.

Read your work carefully and correct any mistakes. Then show your *Gesture Guide* to other students.

Was he the first president?

Talking about past events (1)
Past simple: *be*

1 OPENER

Look at the pictures in the quiz.
What do they show?

2 READING

Do the quiz with another
student.

2.46 Now listen and check your
answers.

3 AFTER READING AND LISTENING

Match the questions with the
answers.

1 Was Abraham Lincoln the
 first president of the USA?
2 Were Armstrong and Aldrin
 the first people on the moon?
3 Was Salvador Dalí from
 Spain?
4 Was Marie Curie the first
 woman to win a Nobel Prize?
5 Was Venus Williams a
 Wimbledon champion at the
 age of 17?
6 Was Brazil the host country
 of the 2008 Olympic Games?
7 Were the Incas from Mexico?
8 Was Pompeii a Roman town?

a Yes, he was.
b No, he wasn't.
c Yes, she was.
d No, she wasn't.
e Yes, it was.
f No, it wasn't.
g Yes, they were.
h No, they weren't.

Your response Which
questions were easy? Which
were more difficult?

Extension Write one or
two similar quiz questions
– make sure you know the
right answers. Then give
your questions to your
teacher and have a class
quiz.

QUIZ *How much do you know about people and places? Find out here! Complete the sentences with A, B or C.*

1 The first president of the USA
was ...
A John F Kennedy.
B Abraham Lincoln.
C George Washington.

2 The first people on the moon
were ...
A Armstrong and Aldrin.
B Lennon and McCartney.
C Tenzing and Hillary.

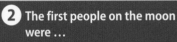

3 The artist Salvador Dalí was
from ...
A France.
B Italy.
C Spain.

4 The first woman to win a
Nobel Prize was ...
A Marie Curie.
B JK Rowling.
C Oprah Winfrey.

5 At the age of 17, ... was a
Wimbledon tennis champion.
A Kim Clijsters
B Maria Sharapova
C Venus Williams

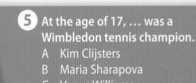

6 The host country of the 2008
Olympic Games was ...
A Australia.
B China.
C Russia.

7 The Incas were from ...
A Brazil.
B Mexico.
C Peru.

8 Pompeii was a Roman ...
A castle.
B town.
C volcano.

4 VOCABULARY

Where were the students at five o'clock yesterday? Read the clues and complete the chart with these places.

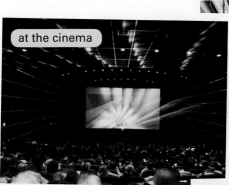

at the cinema

at the shopping centre

in the park

in a café

on the beach

Name	Place
Adam	
Emily	
Jake	
Katya	
Pierre	
Ruby	
Teresa	

Clues

One of the boys was at the cinema.
A boy and a girl were on the beach.
The Russian girl was at the shopping centre.
Teresa wasn't on the beach.
Emily was with Jake.
The English boy was in a café.
Jake wasn't at the cinema.
Teresa and Katya were together.
Adam's sister was in the park.

Now ask and answer.

> Where was Adam at five o'clock yesterday?

> He was …

> Who was in the park?

5 PRONUNCIATION

🔘 2.47 Listen and repeat.

> **Weak form** /wəz/
> Where was Adam's sister?
> She was in the park.
> **Strong form** /wɒz/
> Was she on the beach?
> No, she wasn't.

Now listen and decide: weak or strong?

1 It was five o'clock.
2 Was he in a café?
3 Yes, he was.
4 Who was at the cinema?

6 SPEAKING

Ask and answer questions about different times yesterday. Use the places in exercise 4 to help you.

A Where were you yesterday at noon? Were you in the park?
B No, I wasn't. I was at home/at school/at X's house.
A Who were you with?
B I was with X./I was on my own.

7 WRITING

Write sentences about where you were and who you were with at different times last weekend: in the morning, at noon, in the afternoon/evening.

Last Saturday I was at the cinema with my brother at six o'clock in the evening.

LANGUAGE WORKOUT

Complete.

Past simple: *be*

Affirmative	**Negative**
I/he/she/it **was**	I/he/she/it **wasn't**
we/you/they **were**	we/you/they _____

Questions	**Short answers**
Was I?/**Were** we?	Yes, you **were**.
	No, you **weren't**.
_____ he/she/it?	Yes, he/she/it _____.
	No, he/she/it _____.
_____ they?	Yes, they _____.
	No, they _____.

Contractions _____ = was not
weren't = _____

▶**Answers and Practice**
Language File page 119

Greenland

The Vikings liked music

Talking about past events (2)
Past simple: affirmative

N O R T H
A M E R I C A

Newfoundland

1 OPENER

Look at the map and find these names.
Which five names are continents?

A T L A N T I C   O C E A N

> **Word Bank** Continents and countries
>
> Africa   Asia   Denmark   Europe   France
> Greenland   Iceland   Ireland   Italy   North America
> Norway   Russia   Spain   South America   Sweden

2 READING

🔘 2.48 Read *The Vikings*. What is the most surprising
information in the text?

3 AFTER READING

True or false? Correct the false sentences.

1 The Vikings came from Norway, Sweden
   and Denmark.
2 They went to Britain a thousand years ago.
3 Viking ships were very small.
4 The Vikings played musical instruments.
5 They drank coffee.
6 Viking men wore skirts and trousers.
7 Some Vikings went to Africa.
8 Others sailed west to South America.

Your response What else do you know about
the Vikings? Were they in your country?

4 PRONUNCIATION

🔘 2.49 Listen and write the past simple regular verbs
in the correct column.

> crossed   discovered   liked   played   sailed
> started   visited   wanted   watched

/d/	/t/	/ɪd/
discovered	*crossed*	*started*

Now listen and check. Repeat the words.

5 GAME

Look at the map and make True/False statements
about the Vikings. Use *go to*, *sail to*, *visit*.

> The Vikings visited New York.   False!

> They went to Russia.   True!

The Vikings

The Vikings came from Scandinavia –
Norway, Sweden and Denmark. They were
strong and tall, with fair hair and blue eyes.
The word Viking means pirate, and the
Vikings sailed to Britain over 1,200 years
ago – they wanted to steal gold, silver and
land. They had fantastic ships which carried
up to 200 people!

In the 1970s, archaeologists in Britain
found lots of clues about Viking life. We
now know that the Vikings liked music,
and they played board games and dice
games. They ate meat and lots of fish, fruit
and vegetables. They also made bread
and they drank beer. Viking women wore
long dresses, and the men wore shirts and
trousers. And everyone wore jewellery!

The Vikings were great explorers – Britain
wasn't the only country they visited. Some
Vikings went east through Europe to Asia,
or south to Africa. Others sailed west and
lived in Iceland, Greenland and even North
America. A Viking called Leif Eriksson
crossed the Atlantic 1,000 years ago and
discovered North America 500 years before
Christopher Columbus!

S O U T H
A M E R I C A

Iceland
· Reykjavik

ARCTIC OCEAN

Norway

Sweden Finland

NORTH SEA

Ireland
Dublin York
Britain Denmark
London Hamburg
Paris
Nantes Prague
France Kracow
EUROPE
Spain Italy
· Lisbon
· Seville Rome
· Cadiz

Novgorod

Russia

Kiev

BLACK SEA

Constantinople

ASIA

CASPIAN SEA

MEDITERRANEAN SEA

AFRICA

Alexandria · Jerusalem
· Baghdad
Egypt

6 LISTENING

🔘 2.50 Listen to Katya and Pierre and complete the chart with these phrases.

a café   the cinema   computer games   a dress   a DVD   an ice cream
his/her parents   a pizza   a shirt and jeans   his/her sister   tennis   TV

Yesterday ...	Katya	Pierre	
wore			
went to			
had			
played			
watched			
phoned			

Now talk about Katya and Pierre.

Yesterday Katya wore ...   And Pierre wore ...

7 SPEAKING

Tell another student what you did yesterday using the verbs in the chart. Complete the chart for your partner.

Extension Play *Past Simple Challenge*.

walk   walked

8 WRITING

Write an email to a friend about what you did yesterday.

Hi!
Yesterday was a busy day! In the morning I played tennis with my friend Monika.

Extension Write three true and two false sentences about what you did yesterday. Show the sentences to another student. Can he/she guess which are false?

LANGUAGE WORKOUT

Complete.

Past simple: affirmative
Regular verbs
The Vikings sail**ed** to Britain.
The Vikings like**d** music.

We add *ed* to most regular verbs:
cross____   discover____   play____
sail____   visit____
We add *d* to regular verbs ending in *e*:
like____   live____
Verbs ending in a consonant + *y* change *y* to *i* and add *ed*:
carry – carr**ied**

Irregular verbs
The Vikings **came** from Scandinavia.
They **had** fantastic ships.

Find the past tense of these irregular verbs in the text.
come _____   drink _____
eat _____   find _____   go _____
have _____   make _____
wear _____

►**Answers and Practice**
Language File pages 119–120
Irregular Verbs page 127

Did he say sorry?

Asking about past events
Past simple: negative, questions and short answers

1 OPENER

Look at the photo. Guess: What are Teresa and Pierre talking about?
Choose one of these adjectives to describe how Pierre is feeling.

Word Bank Feelings

angry   cross   happy   sad   scared   surprised   worried

2 READING

2.51 Read the dialogue. What's the problem?

The group went by minibus to Devil's Dyke, near Brighton.

TERESA   What's the matter, Pierre? Everything OK?

PIERRE   Not really. Adam borrowed my new camera and then he lost it.

TERESA   Lost it? How did he lose it?

PIERRE   I don't know – he left it somewhere.

TERESA   Oh no! How did you feel about that?

PIERRE   Well, to be honest, I was quite cross. But I didn't say anything to him.

TERESA   Did he say sorry?

PIERRE   No, he didn't apologise. And he didn't even seem worried.

TERESA   Where is he now? Where did he go?

PIERRE   He went back to the minibus.

TERESA   Oh look! Here he comes! Hi, Adam! Did you find Pierre's camera?

ADAM   No, I didn't. Anyway, it's only a camera, Pierre. You can always buy a new one.

PIERRE   What do you mean, buy a new one?!

ADAM   Don't get angry! Here it is. Joke! I found it on the minibus.

TERESA   That was a silly joke, Adam.

PIERRE   Well, everything's all right now. I'm sorry I got angry.

TERESA   Let's forget about it. There's a new Dracula movie on at the cinema. Why don't we all go tonight?

3 AFTER READING

Answer the questions.

1   Who lent Adam a camera?
2   Did Adam say sorry?
3   Where did Adam go?
4   Who got angry?
5   Where did Adam find the camera?
6   Did Teresa think Adam's joke was funny?
7   Who apologised to Adam?
8   What did Teresa want to do?

Your response Did you think Adam's joke was funny?

4 READING

Read and choose the best words.

The group returned to Brighton after their visit to Devil's Dyke. They agreed to meet outside the cinema at 7pm. After breakfast/dinner Adam cycled straight to the cinema and Pierre drove/walked through The Lanes. The Lanes are a part of Brighton with lots of old shops and houses. Pierre stopped and looked in a shop window/door.

Then he saw a girl. She carried/wore a long white dress. It was Teresa! She was twenty metres away, but Pierre knew it was Teresa. 'Where did she get that dress from?' Pierre thought.

'Hi, Teresa!' he shouted. The girl looked at Pierre and smiled. Then she walked away. Pierre ran after her. 'Hey! Stop!' he laughed/shouted, but the girl didn't stop – she went into an old house. Pierre ran in after her. The girl was at the top of the stairs. Then she danced/turned and looked down at him. She took two steps forward.

Pierre was scared. He closed his eyes/hands. But when he opened them again, there was no one there! Where was Teresa?

Pierre called/talked Adam on his mobile. 'Hi, Adam. It's Pierre. There's something I don't understand. I'm in an old house in The Lanes. And Teresa was here in a long white dress – but now I can't find her.'

'You're wrong, Pierre,' Adam said. 'Teresa is with me, outside the cinema/park.'

So who did Pierre see in The Lanes?

5 LISTENING

(O) 2.52 Listen and check your answers to exercise 4.

Now ask and answer.

> Did Pierre drive through The Lanes?

> No, he didn't. He walked through The Lanes.

> Did he look in a shop window?

> Yes, he did.

> **Extension** Close your book and tell another student what happened to Pierre in the Lanes.

6 PRONUNCIATION

(O) 2.53 Listen and repeat.

| high | honest | knew | thought |
| tonight | two | white | wrong |

Now cross out the silent letters.

hig̶h̶

7 SPEAKING

Ask other students questions about last night.

> Did you watch TV last night?

> Yes, I did.

1 watch TV
2 listen to the radio
3 have dinner with your family
4 play a musical instrument
5 play a board game
6 do your homework
7 phone a friend
8 send an email
9 wash your hair
10 go to bed late

> **Extension** Write about five students.
> *Rafael didn't watch TV last night.*

8 WRITING

Write a short dialogue between two friends. Begin like this:

A *I saw a ghost last night!*
B *I don't believe you! Where did you see it?*

LANGUAGE WORKOUT

Complete.

Past simple
Negative
He **didn't** apologise.
He _____ seem worried.
I _____ say anything to him.

Questions	**Short answers**
Did Adam find the camera?	Yes, he **did**.
Did you find Pierre's camera?	No, I _____.
_____ Pierre apologise?	Yes, he _____.
_____ they visit Devil's Dyke?	Yes, they _____.

For short answers we use the past simple forms *did/didn't* after *I/you/he/she/it/we/they*.
Regular and irregular verbs form the negative and questions in the same way.

►**Answers and Practice**
Language File pages 119–120

4 Integrated Skills
Telling a story

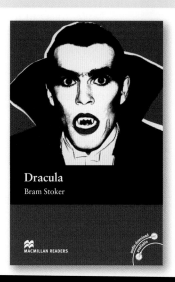

Dracula
Bram Stoker

MACMILLAN READERS

Introduction

In the 15th century, a real prince called Dracula lived in a castle in Transylvania (now part of Romania). People thought that Prince Dracula was a vampire. They believed that vampires attacked people at night and drank their blood. Then these people also became vampires. There were lots of stories about Prince Dracula. In 1897, Bram Stoker wrote his famous story.

Bram Stoker's Dracula

An Englishman called Jonathan Harker visited Castle Dracula in 1875. But strange things happened in the castle, and Dracula was a strange man. Why didn't he eat? Why didn't he sleep at night? Why did Harker never see Dracula in the day? Harker was scared and he wanted to leave the castle. He thought about England and his girlfriend, Mina. But Dracula wanted Harker to stay …

1 OPENER

Look at the cover of the book. What is the story about?

2 READING

🔘 2.54 Read the introduction and the first part of Bram Stoker's story, and answer the questions.

1 Where did Dracula live?
2 What did vampires drink?
3 When did Bram Stoker write *Dracula*?
4 When did Jonathan Harker go to Castle Dracula?
5 What was strange about Dracula?
6 Why did Harker want to leave the castle?
7 What was the name of Harker's girlfriend?

3 LISTENING

🔘 2.55 Listen to the second part of the story and number pictures A–D in the right order.

4 SPEAKING

Look at the pictures and say what happened in the second part of the story.

5 WRITING

Complete the last part of the story with *and, but, then*.

Mina and Lucy went back to London, __1__ Lucy became very ill __2__ died. She was now a vampire!

Finally, Harker escaped from Dracula's castle __3__ he came back to England. __4__ he saw Dracula in London! Harker __5__ Mina asked a friend, Professor Van Helsing, for help. Van Helsing guessed that Dracula was a vampire. The men decided to find __6__ kill Dracula. __7__ where was he?

One night Dracula visited Mina __8__ kissed her neck. She started to change into a vampire! __9__ Van Helsing found out that Dracula was on a boat to Transylvania. Harker, Van Helsing __10__ Mina went to Transylvania by train. Now Mina was very ill __11__ there wasn't a lot of time.

They found Dracula outside his castle – it was almost dark! They killed the vampire __12__ saved Mina's life. Dracula was dead!

🔘 2.56 Now listen and check.

LEARNER INDEPENDENCE

6 Irregular verbs are important in English, so it's a good idea to learn them. Find and write down the past simple forms of the irregular verbs from this lesson.

> become   come   drink   find
> go   see   think   write

You can use the list on page 127 to learn more irregular verbs! Then test another student.

7 Add these sections to your vocabulary notebook.

Continents   Feelings   Transport

8 🔘 2.57 **Phrasebook:** Find these useful expressions in Unit 6. Then listen and repeat.

> What's the matter?
> Everything OK?
> Not really.
> To be honest …
> Here he comes!
> What do you mean?
> Let's forget about it.

Write a short dialogue beginning with one of the questions in the box and ending with one of the other expressions.

PROJECT *Famous explorers*

1 Work in a group and look again at Unit 6 Lesson 2. Then make a list of famous explorers and expeditions. Think about expeditions to the North and South Poles, sailing and flying around the world, and space exploration. Choose one or two explorers or expeditions to write about.

2 Research: Find out information from books or the Internet, and make notes about the explorers/ expeditions, for example:

- Where and when did they go?
- How did they travel?
- What problems were there?
- Were they successful?
- What happened afterwards – what were the results of the expedition?

3 Work together and write about the explorers and expeditions. Read your work carefully and correct any mistakes. Draw pictures or find photos from the Internet. Show your work to the other groups.

Amy Johnson was the first woman to fly alone from England to Australia. She left London on 5th May 1930 in an aeroplane called *Jason*. There were some problems on the 16,000 kilometre flight – she crash-landed in Burma – but on 24th May she finally landed in Darwin in the north of Australia. Then she flew south to Brisbane, but crashed the plane when she landed. As a result of this accident, Johnson met pilot Jim Mollison, who flew her to Sydney and became her husband!

Game *Three in a Line*

- Form three teams: Team A, Team B and Team C.
- Team A chooses a verb square, and says the number. Then Team A asks Team B a question about yesterday with the verb in the past simple. Team B answers and then makes a question for Team C.
- Teams who ask correct questions 'win' the square. The aim of the game is to win three squares in a line (across, down or diagonally).
- Teams who give incorrect answers lose their turn to ask the next question.

> Square 1. Did you borrow anything yesterday?

> Yes, I did. I borrowed a CD.

1 borrow	2 buy	3 eat	4 forget	5 get up
6 go	7 have	8 help	9 learn	10 listen
11 lose	12 phone	13 play	14 read	15 see
16 study	17 talk	18 visit	19 watch	20 write

REVISION

LESSON 1 Look at the completed chart in exercise 4 on page 77. Write sentences saying where the characters were at five o'clock yesterday.

Adam was ...

LESSON 2 Look at the chart in exercise 6 on page 79. Write six sentences each about what Katya and Pierre did yesterday.

Yesterday Katya wore ...

LESSON 3 Look at exercise 4 on page 81. Write sentences about what did and didn't happen.

Pierre didn't drive through The Lanes. He walked through The Lanes.

LESSON 4 Look at the list of irregular verbs on page 127. Cover the *Past simple* column with a piece of paper and write the past simple of all the verbs you know.

EXTENSION

LESSON 1 Write five quiz questions about past events in your country.

Who was/were ...?
What was/were ...?
Where was/were ...?

Ask another student to answer your questions.

LESSON 2 Look at the list of irregular verbs in Language Workout on page 79. Choose six and write a true sentence about yourself with each verb in the past simple.

I came home late yesterday.

LESSON 3 Look at exercise 7 on page 81. Think of questions you can ask about last weekend. Write a short dialogue between you and a friend about what you both did last weekend.

LESSON 4 Look at the pictures on pages 82–83. Imagine you are Mina and write a diary about what happened.

At first, Lucy and I enjoyed our holiday by the sea. But then I became worried.

YOUR CHOICE!

WHICH COUNTRY IS IT?

- Work in a small group.
- On your own, think of a country and make notes about it, for example:

  Where is it?
  How big is it?
  What's the weather like?
  What language(s) do people speak?
  Famous people from the country

- Tell the rest of the group about the country but don't say its name. They try to guess the country.

CONSEQUENCES

- Work in pairs to write stories together. You both need pieces of paper.
- Write a person's name at the top of your paper. Fold the paper to hide the name and exchange papers with your partner. Next, write *met* and another person's name. Fold the paper and exchange it again. Continue writing answers to questions 3–7 and exchange folded papers after each answer.

1 Who? (*Name A*)	5 What did A say?
2 ... met who? (*Name B*)	6 What did B say?
3 Where?	7 What was the
4 When?	consequence?

- Now unfold the papers and read out your stories.

1 Read and complete. For each number 1–12, choose word A, B or C.

'I DIDN'T WAIT – I JUMPED IN!'

A teenager jumped into the River Thames in London yesterday and __1__ the life of a tourist. Jo Andrews was by the river when she __2__ a young man in the water.

18-year-old Jo, who started a new job at a swimming pool two weeks __3__, said, 'The tourist fell out of a boat into the water.'

'He shouted, but he __4__ speak any English. At first no one thought it was a problem. There __5__ lots of people there and they all laughed. Then I heard a shout of "Help!". It was the young man's father,' said Jo, who __6__ at Chelsea Sports Centre. 'The father jumped into the water too, but he __7__ know how to swim.'

'I asked a woman to help me,' Jo said. 'The woman jumped in and swam to the __8__ father. I swam out to the son. His head was underwater. I pulled him up, but then he __9__ down again. It became __10__ difficult to hold him. My jeans got wetter and wetter and they pulled me under the water. I thought I __11__ in the water for a long time, but it was really only two or three minutes.'

People __12__ Jo and together they pulled the young tourist out of the river. 'I didn't wait – I jumped in,' said Jo. Her mum, Jackie, said: 'I'm very pleased. She was wonderful.'

1	**A** save	**B** saves	**C** saved
2	**A** saw	**B** see	**C** sees
3	**A** after	**B** ago	**C** before
4	**A** didn't	**B** doesn't	**C** don't
5	**A** was	**B** wasn't	**C** were
6	**A** is working	**B** work	**C** works
7	**A** didn't	**B** doesn't	**C** don't
8	**A** tourist	**B** tourist's	**C** tourists
9	**A** goes	**B** going	**C** went
10	**A** more	**B** many	**C** much
11	**A** am	**B** was	**C** were
12	**A** help	**B** helping	**C** helped

2 Complete with the correct form of the present simple or present continuous.

1 Pierre usually _____ to the cinema on Friday. (go)
2 It's 7.30 – Teresa and Katya _____ breakfast. (have)
4 Emily's cousin _____ on a boat this summer. (work)
5 She _____ to the news on the radio every day. (listen)
5 The exchange students _____ Brighton at the moment. (visit)
6 _____ you _____ the party? (enjoy)
7 I _____ your phone number. (not know)
8 How many languages _____ you _____? (speak)

3 Write questions and answers.

magazine/Adam
Whose magazine is this? It's Adam's.

1 cat/Teresa   4 jeans/Katya
2 sunglasses/Pierre   5 umbrella/the teacher
3 mobile phone/Mr Ward 6 CDs/my friend

4 Write sentences.

her   *They're her earrings.*
        They're hers.

1 his   2 our   3 their

4 her   5 my   6 your

5 Write sentences using comparative adjectives.

Spain/hot/than Britain
Spain is hotter than Britain.

1 Florida/sunny/than New York
2 Japanese/difficult/than English
3 A Ferrari/expensive/than a Fiat
4 Mexico City/big/than Rio de Janeiro
5 Mount Everest/high/than K2
6 Tom Cruise/famous/than me

6 Ask and answer.

television/1920 ✗

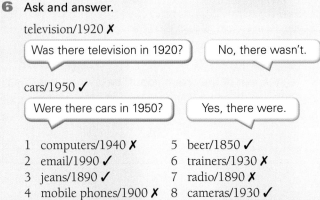

Was there television in 1920?   No, there wasn't.

cars/1950 ✓

Were there cars in 1950?   Yes, there were.

1 computers/1940 ✗   5 beer/1850 ✓
2 email/1990 ✓   6 trainers/1930 ✗
3 jeans/1890 ✓   7 radio/1890 ✗
4 mobile phones/1900 ✗ 8 cameras/1930 ✓

7 Write the past simple of these regular verbs under the correct sound.

> answer ask check decide enjoy kiss
> listen repeat shout smile talk wait

/d/	/t/	/ɪd/
answered	*asked*	*decided*

2.58 Now listen and check.

8 Complete with the past simple of these verbs.

> cook find know play run sail see visit

1 The Vikings _____ to America a thousand years ago.
2 Adam and Ruby _____ pasta for dinner last night.
3 We _____ a film about Dracula on TV a week ago.
4 Emily _____ five kilometres this morning.
5 Mr Ward _____ New York last year.
6 Jake _____ basketball yesterday.
7 I _____ 20 euros in the street a minute ago!
8 You _____ the answers to all the questions!

9 Ask and answer.

> Did Teresa phone home?   Yes, she did.

> Did she phone Adam?   No, she didn't.

1 Teresa/phone home ✓/Adam ✗
2 Pierre/write a letter ✗/an email ✓
3 Emily/wear a jacket✓/a dress ✗
4 Katya and Teresa/go the café ✗/the shopping centre ✓
5 Jake and Adam/play tennis ✓/basketball ✗
6 Diana/listen to CDs ✗/the radio ✓

Now write sentences.

Teresa phoned home. She didn't phone Adam.

VOCABULARY

10 Complete with eight of these words.

> blood coast dress explorer hill
> news storm sun temperature train

1 It's a beautiful day and the _____ is shining.
2 She wore a nice _____ for the party.
3 It's very hot – what's the _____?
4 Christopher Columbus was a famous _____.
5 Vampires drink people's _____.
6 We walked up the _____ to the church.
7 I watched the _____ on TV.
8 You can go from London to Brighton by _____.

11 Match these words with their definitions.

> apologise cross *adj* huge journalist
> noon nurse ship short terrible wet

1 midday
2 say sorry
3 opposite of *long* or *tall*
4 big boat
5 quite angry
6 opposite of *dry*
7 very bad
8 very big
9 someone who looks after people who are ill
10 someone who writes news stories

12 Match the verbs in list A with the words and phrases in list B.

	A	B
1	ask	at someone
2	close	a boat
3	drive	maths
4	fly	your eyes
5	fold	for help
6	go	a plane
7	sail	to sleep
8	shout	a car
9	teach	your arms

LEARNER INDEPENDENCE
SELF ASSESSMENT

Look back at Lessons 1–3 in Units 5 and 6.

How good are you at …?	✓Fine	? Not sure
1 Talking about regular activities Workbook p54 exercises 1 and 2	☐	☐
2 Talking about what people are doing now Workbook p54 exercise 3	☐	☐
3 Talking about possessions Workbook pp56–57 exercises 1, 2 and 5	☐	☐
4 Making comparisons Workbook pp58–59 exercises 1–5	☐	☐
5 Talking about past events Workbook p66 exercises 1–3, pp68–69 exercises 1–6 and p70 exercise 1	☐	☐
6 Asking about past events Workbook p67 exercises 4–6 and pp70–71 exercises 2–4	☐	☐

Not sure? Have a look at Language File pages 117–120 and do the Workbook exercise(s) again.

Now write an example for 1–6

1 *Adam's father flies planes to South-east Asia.*

87

PREVIEW

UNITS 7-8

COMMUNICATIVE AIMS
LEARNING HOW TO ...

1 Talk about future plans and intentions
2 Ask for and give reasons
3 Talk about likes and dislikes
4 Make comparisons
5 Make and accept/decline offers
6 Talk about money and prices
7 Talk about possessions
8 Ask for agreement

TOPICS AND VOCABULARY

Accident and emergency
Leisure activities
Animals
Adjectives
Travel
Kitchen equipment
Food and drink
Possessions
Invitations and thanks
Life in another country

A

INVITATION
❈ ❈ ❈
The Campbell family invite
all the NFI Exchange Students
to a Barbecue Party to celebrate the end of the visit.

Sunday 24th July   2–6pm

❈ ❈ ❈

8 Hill Street, Lewes   RSVP Tel 837921

B

They're going to X-ray his leg.

---

1 Match the pictures (A–F) with six items in the Topics and Vocabulary box.

2 Put the words into categories.

> Animals
> Food
> Possessions

computer game
cow whale fruit
games console
potato skateboard camera phone
cake
blu-ray disc
dog egg cat
horse rice

3 🔘 3.01 Listen to extracts 1–3 from Units 7 and 8. Match them with these topics.

A Leisure activities
B Food and drink
C Animals

C Would you like a sandwich?

D I'm going to visit my aunt and uncle in Kenya.

E

Orlando Bloom really likes skydiving.

I haven't got a games console.

F

4 Do the Animal Facts Quiz with two other students.

ANIMAL FACTS QUIZ TRUE OR FALSE?

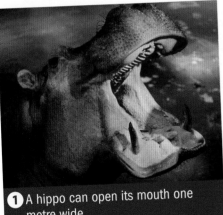

1 A hippo can open its mouth one metre wide.

2 Dolphins can sleep with one eye open.

3 Owls are the only birds which can see the colour blue.

4 Penguins are the only birds which can swim but can't fly.

5 Dogs can hear sounds that people can't.

Believe it or not!

Like people and dolphins, elephants can recognise themselves in a mirror.

Answers to Quiz: All the facts are true.

Talking about future plans and intentions
Asking for and giving reasons
going to
Why? because ...

1 OPENER

Look at the photo. Guess: What is Pierre telling Ruby and Adam?

2 READING

🔘 3.02 Read the dialogue. What's the problem?

ADAM   Are you OK, Pierre? Why are you looking worried?

PIERRE   Because there's a text from my mum. It's about my dad.

ADAM   What's wrong with him?

PIERRE   He had an accident at work – he hurt his leg – and they called an ambulance.

ADAM   That's terrible. Is he going to be all right?

PIERRE   Well, he's in hospital and they're going to X-ray his leg. But my mother wants me to go back to Geneva.

ADAM   What are you going to do?

PIERRE   What do you think?

RUBY   Oh, no! You aren't going to be at the barbecue on Sunday!

ADAM   Ruby!

PIERRE   Excuse me, I'm going to phone home now.

3 AFTER READING

Match the questions with the answers. There is one wrong answer.

1 Why is Pierre worried?
2 Where is Pierre's father?
3 What does Pierre's mother want?
4 Why is Ruby unhappy?
5 What is Pierre going to do?

a He's going to phone his mother.
b Because she wants Pierre to be at the barbecue.
c He's in hospital.
d Because he's going to go to the barbecue.
e Because his father had an accident at work.
f She wants Pierre to go back to Geneva.

Your response Imagine you are Pierre. What are you going to say when you phone home?

4 LISTENING

🔘 3.03 Listen to Pierre and decide: true or false? Correct the false sentences.

1 Pierre talked to his father.
2 His father isn't going to stay in hospital.
3 His father wants him to go home early.
4 Pierre is going to stay in Brighton.
5 Ruby isn't going to be very happy.

5 SPEAKING

Imagine you get these messages. Discuss what you are going to do with another student.

1

Someone called Julie phoned from the BBC. She wants you to be on TV! It's a programme about teenage life. Please ring back.

What are you going to do first?

A Tell all your friends.

B Go out and buy new clothes.

C Phone and say yes.

2

12:23

The police phoned – they want to speak to you about your friend Lisa. She's not at home or at school and her parents are worried. Mum x

You know where your friend is and she's OK. What are you going to do?

A Tell the police.

B Tell your friend's parents.

C Speak to your friend.

3

| Get Mail | Write | Contacts | Reply | Forward | Delete | Print |

You won the competition! The prize is a week's holiday in New York for you and a friend. Can you let us know who is going to go with you?

You have two good friends and you don't know which friend to take to New York. What are you going to do?

A Go to New York on your own.

B Tell your two friends the problem.

C Choose one friend and not tell the other.

Extension Discuss these situations with two other students. What are you going to do?

You find a new mobile in the street.

You get a present that you don't like.

You miss the school bus.

6 PRONUNCIATION

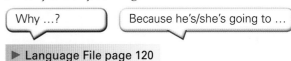 **3.04** Listen and repeat. Mark the stress.

> accident   ambulance   barbecue   holiday
> hospital   police   programme   terrible   worried

Which word is different?

7 GAME

Play *Guess the reason!*

1 Why is Pierre wearing shorts?

2 Why is Adam turning on the computer?

3 Why is Teresa buying a ticket?

4 Why is Mr Ward learning Portuguese?

5 Why is Emily running?

> Why …?   Because he's/she's going to …

▶ Language File page 120

 **3.05** Now listen and check.

8 SPEAKING

Make a list of five things you're going to do after school today. Then ask questions to find other students who are going to do the same thing.

> Are you going to watch a DVD?   No, I'm not. Are you going to listen to music?
>
> Yes, I am

Now ask five students what they are going to do in the summer holidays.

> What are you going to do in the summer holidays?   I'm going to go to Italy. What are you going to do?

Extension Write sentences about what you and other students are going to do after school today.

9 WRITING

Reply to this question from your English epal.

What are you and your friends going to do in the summer holidays?

LANGUAGE WORKOUT

Complete.

***going to*: future plans and intentions**

I _____ going _____ phone home.

They _____ going _____ X-ray his leg.

You _____ not _____ to be at the barbecue.

_____ he _____ to be all right?

What _____ you _____ _____ do?

▶**Answers and Practice**
Language File page 120

2

She loves skateboarding

**Talking about likes and dislikes
Verb + gerund**

1 OPENER

Which activities can you see in the photos? Choose from these words.

Word Bank Leisure activities

dancing   drawing   fishing   knitting   painting
playing chess   playing the guitar   playing ice hockey
riding   rollerblading   sailing   skateboarding
skydiving   snowboarding   surfing   swimming

2 READING

🔘 3.06   Read *What do the stars like doing in their free time?* on page 93. Which is the most surprising fact in the article?

3 AFTER READING

True or false? Correct the false sentences.

1   Avril Lavigne really likes snowboarding.
2   Avril Lavigne doesn't enjoy playing video games.
3   Johnny Depp doesn't mind dancing.
4   Cameron Díaz and Uma Thurman don't like knitting.
5   Orlando Bloom loves skydiving.
6   Robert Pattinson hates snowboarding.

Your response Think of other stars and guess what their leisure activities are.

4 PRONUNCIATION

🔘 3.07   Listen and repeat.

/aɪ/ **dive**	/ɪ/ **swim**
like	knit
ride	sing

Write these words in the correct column.

fish   give   mind   nice   sit   thing   time   write

Now listen and check.

Extension Think of four more words for each sound and write two lists. Compare your lists with other students.

What do the stars like doing in their free time?

Avril Lavigne – the Canadian singer of Sk8er Boi (pronounced 'Skater Boy') – loves skateboarding. She also likes playing video games in her free time.

Johnny Depp likes reading, playing the guitar and painting. But the star of *Pirates of the Caribbean* hates dancing.

Lots of celebrities enjoy knitting, including Cameron Díaz, Julia Roberts and Uma Thurman.

Orlando Bloom really enjoys skydiving. He knows it's dangerous but he doesn't mind jumping out of a plane at 5,000 metres. He also likes snowboarding and surfing.

Twilight star Robert Pattinson loves snowboarding, skiing and football. He also likes reading.

5 LISTENING

3.08 Listen to Katya and Adam and complete the chart.

like 😊   don't mind 😐   hate ☹️

	Katya	Adam
skateboarding	☹️	😊
painting		
riding		
swimming		
dancing		
playing chess		

Now talk about Katya and Adam.

> Katya hates skateboarding.

> Adam likes skateboarding.

6 SPEAKING

Ask three students about leisure activities in the Word Bank in exercise 1. Note down their answers.

> Do you like …?

> Yes, I do/I love it.

> I don't mind it.

> No, I don't/I hate it.

Extension Use your notes to write about two of the students you interviewed.

7 WRITING

Write to an epal about your likes and dislikes.

I love skateboarding, but I don't like rollerblading.

LANGUAGE WORKOUT

Complete.

Verb + gerund
I love skateboard**ing**.
She likes play___ video games.
We enjoy swim**ming**.
They like knit___.
He doesn't like danc___.
He doesn't mind jump___ out of a plane.
What do they like do___?

▶**Answers and Practice**
Language File page 120

93

3 The most dangerous animal

Making comparisons (2)
Superlative adjectives (*-est, most*)

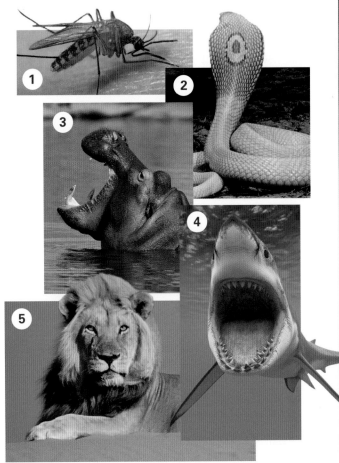

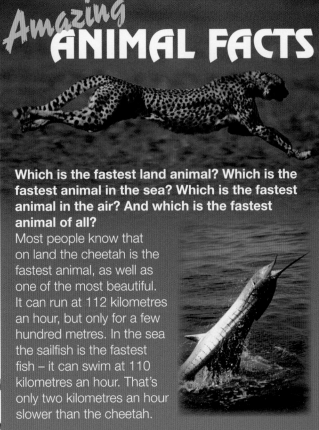

Amazing ANIMAL FACTS

Which is the fastest land animal? Which is the fastest animal in the sea? Which is the fastest animal in the air? And which is the fastest animal of all?

Most people know that on land the cheetah is the fastest animal, as well as one of the most beautiful. It can run at 112 kilometres an hour, but only for a few hundred metres. In the sea the sailfish is the fastest fish – it can swim at 110 kilometres an hour. That's only two kilometres an hour slower than the cheetah.

1 OPENER

Match these animals with photos 1–5. Which do you think is the most dangerous?

> **Word Bank** Animals
>
> hippo   lion   mosquito   shark   snake

2 READING

3.09 Read *Amazing Animal Facts* and find the answers to the four questions in the first paragraph.

3 AFTER READING

Complete.

1 The _____ land animal can run at 112 km/h.
2 The fastest _____ can swim at 110 km/h.
3 When it dives, the _____ is the _____ of all.
4 The Indian cobra isn't the _____ dangerous animal in the world.
5 Mosquitoes are _____ because their bites can give you malaria.
6 That's why mosquitoes are the _____ _____ animals in the world.

Your response Which animals are you scared of?

In the air the falcon is the fastest bird, with a speed of 100 kilometres an hour in level flight. But when it dives down it flies at an amazing 389 kilometres an hour. So the cheetah is a little faster than the sailfish, but the fastest of all is the falcon.

And which is the most dangerous animal in the world?

We're all scared of sharks, but they don't kill many people. And hippos kill more people than lions. In India and Sri Lanka the most dangerous animal is a snake – the Indian cobra. This snake kills over 50,000 people a year. But the most dangerous animal in the world is an insect – the mosquito. Mosquito bites can give you malaria. The World Health Organisation says that about 250 million people a year get malaria. One million people, mostly children in hot countries, die of the disease. Scientists say that malaria killed half the people who ever lived.

4 VOCABULARY

Match the words for animals with the pictures.

> **Word Bank** Animals
>
> cat cow dog elephant giraffe horse
> monkey octopus parrot penguin
> polar bear rabbit sheep tiger whale

1

2

3

4

5

5 SPEAKING

Talk about each group of pictures in exercise 4 using the superlative of these adjectives.

> **Word Bank** Adjectives
>
> beautiful/ugly big/small dangerous/friendly
> exciting/boring fast/slow tall/short

> Group 1: The elephant is the biggest.
> And the tiger is the smallest.

6 PRONUNCIATION

🔘 3.10 Listen and repeat.

/f/

The fastest flying falcon
flies faster than the
fastest flying fish.

7 GAME

Play *Best/Worst in the World*. A chooses a category and B makes a sentence using *best* or *worst*.

> **Categories**
>
> band book film film star football team
> singer song TV programme

> Football team.

> Manchester United is the worst team in the world.

> **Extension** Make sentences for four of these categories with both *best* and *worst*.
>
> car computer game footballer mobile phone
> racing driver skier tennis player

8 SPEAKING

Do a class survey. What kinds of pets do the class have? What are the most popular pets and what is the most popular pet's name?

> Do you have a pet? What's it called?

> **Extension** Repeat the survey with your family and friends, and write the results.

9 WRITING

Write a paragraph giving the results of your class survey.

The most popular pets in our class are dogs. The second most popular pets are ...

LANGUAGE WORKOUT

Complete.

Adjective	Superlative
fast	the fast**est**
slow	the _____
strange	the strang**est**
big	the big**gest**
hot	the hot_____
dry	the dr**iest**
friendly	the friendl_____
dangerous	the **most** dangerous
beautiful	the _____ _____
Irregular	
good	the **best**
bad	the **worst**

Short adjectives end in *est* and _____ adjectives take _____ in front of them.

▶ **Answers and Practice**
Language File pages 120–121

File Edit History Bookmarks Print View Window Help

http://www.askatravelquestion.com

ASK A TRAVEL QUESTION
QUESTIONS

1 I want to go on a whale-watching holiday. But I can only find holidays in North and South America and South Africa. Where's the best place to see whales in Europe?

2 My class is doing a project on India. When is the best time to travel there?

3 I love learning new skills when I'm on holiday. This year I want to learn how to surf. Where's the best place to learn? Don't say Australia or Hawaii!

4 I'm going to visit my aunt and uncle in Kenya this summer and I'm worried about malaria. What's the best medicine to take? I know some malaria medicines make you feel ill. What do you suggest?

5 My father works in New York and I'm going to see him this summer. I love riding and we're going to go on a cowboy ranch holiday. He says I can choose where we go. Where's the best ranch for teenagers and adults?

File Edit History Bookmarks Print View Window He

http://www.askatravelquestion.com

ANSWERS

A You get malaria from a mosquito bite. Make sure that mosquitoes don't bite you! There are a lot of different medicines for malaria. Your doctor knows which medicine is best for the country you're going to visit.

B There are lots of places to choose from in the USA. We had great fun last year at a place in Aspen in Colorado. It's a working ranch and you can help the cowboys. The riding lessons are really good and the food is excellent.

C It's a big country so there isn't one best time. But it's probably best from October to mid April. Summer is from March to June. There is a lot of rain from July to September. October is warm and winter is from November to February.

D In Europe one of the best places is Newquay in the south-west of England. There are some good schools there and it isn't very expensive. The surf and beaches are great – it's where they have international surfing championships.

E There are plenty of good whale-watching holidays in Europe, from Greece or Spain to Scandinavia. You can even see whales – and dolphins – off the coasts of Scotland, Wales and Ireland.

1 OPENER

Look at the website message board. What is the topic?

2 READING

3.11 Read the messages and match the questions with the answers. Then listen and check.

3 LISTENING

You are going to listen to a radio travel programme. First, read the notes below and guess which highlighted words you are going to hear.

Caller 1

QUESTION: Samantha wants to learn/teach Spanish. Someone told her that Cuba is a good/bad place to study.

ANSWER: Cuba is fine. The best/worst way is to live with a Spanish-speaking family.

Caller 2

QUESTION: Will wants to know about the weather/winter in Africa/Australia.

ANSWER: Visit this website: _____.

Caller 3

QUESTION: Terry is going to India/Italy. It's his first/second visit and he likes going to beaches/museums.

ANSWER: The food is the best/worst in the world. Start/Finish in Naples and go to two/three other cities.

3.12 Now listen to the programme and check. Complete the website address.

4 SPEAKING

Look again at the notes in exercise 3 and the questions and answers on the website. Then role play three conversations on a radio phone-in programme. One student is the caller and the other is the travel expert. The caller asks questions about your country:

1 about learning your language
2 about the weather
3 about which places to visit

Caller	Expert
Say your name and where you are calling from.	
	Reply.
Ask your question.	
	Reply.
Say thank you.	
	Say goodbye.

5 WRITING

Look at the messages in exercise 2. Write three questions asking for travel information about countries you want to visit.

LEARNER INDEPENDENCE

6 Classroom English: Put these words in the right order to make sentences. You can use the sentences to ask your teacher or another student for help.

1 now suggest you what do I do?
2 best what do exercise is way the to this?
3 you please it can spell?
4 turn my it is now?
5 word what mean this does?
6 word pronounce you do this how?
7 dictionary use I can please a?
8 me correct is excuse this?

7 Add these sections to your vocabulary notebook. Write at least four words in each section.

Health and illness
Animals
Leisure activities (add to your list from Unit 3)

8 **3.13** **Phrasebook:** Find these useful expressions in Unit 7. Then listen and repeat.

> Are you OK?
> What's wrong with him?
> That's terrible.
> What are you going to do?
> What do you think?
> Please ring back.
> I love it.
> I don't mind it.
> I hate it.
> What do you suggest?

Now write your own answers to four of the questions in the box.

LANGUAGE LINKS

Here are four different airport signs in English, French, German and Spanish. Match the signs which have the same meaning. Are any of the words like each other?

Baggage   Arrivals   Check-in   Departures

Arrivées   Bagages   Départs   Enregistrement

Abfertigung   Abflug   Ankunft   Gepäck

Equipaje   Facturación   Llegadas   Salidas

SKETCH *Superlative Holidays!*

🔘 3.14   Read and listen.

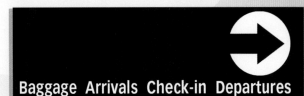

TRAVEL AGENT	Good morning, can I help you?
CUSTOMER	Yes, please. I want to book a holiday.
TRAVEL AGENT	What kind of holiday? The coldest, the most dangerous, the most exciting?
CUSTOMER	What's the most exciting holiday?
TRAVEL AGENT	Two weeks' skydiving.
CUSTOMER	Isn't that the most dangerous one?
TRAVEL AGENT	Oh no! The most dangerous holiday is two weeks' skydiving over a sea full of sharks.
CUSTOMER	No. I don't really like flying.
TRAVEL AGENT	Well, what about the coldest holiday? You stay in an igloo in the Arctic.
CUSTOMER	But I like warm weather.
TRAVEL AGENT	OK, what about the hottest holiday? You ride a camel across the Sahara Desert.
CUSTOMER	No, that's too hot. What else is there?
TRAVEL AGENT	Let's see. There's the longest holiday – a trip to Mars!
CUSTOMER	But I only have two weeks. And I don't have a lot of money.
TRAVEL AGENT	Then I think the best thing for you is the cheapest holiday.
CUSTOMER	What's that?
TRAVEL AGENT	You stay at home!

Now act out the sketch in pairs.

Game   *Find someone who ...*

Ask other students questions and complete the chart.

> Do you like being underwater?

Name	Find someone who ...
	doesn't like being underwater.
	enjoys ironing.
	likes singing in the shower.
	hates getting up early.
	likes wearing green.
	doesn't like touching snakes.
	enjoys cooking.
	loves eating carrots.

The first person to complete the chart with eight *different* names is the winner.

Limerick

🔘 3.15   Read and listen.

A young kangaroo in Australia
Said 'I'm a terrible failure!
I can't jump at all
'Cause my legs are too small –
I'm the worst kangaroo in Australia!'

REVISION

LESSON 1 Look at the messages in exercise 5 on page 91. What are you going to do? Write your intention for each situation.

1 First I'm going to ...

LESSON 2 Look at the completed chart in exercise 5 on page 93. Write sentences about Katya and Adam's likes and dislikes.

Katya hates skateboarding, but Adam likes it.

LESSON 3 Look at exercise 4 on page 95. Write a sentence about each group of pictures using superlative adjectives.

The giraffe is the tallest, but the tiger is the most beautiful.

LESSON 4 Look at the role play in exercise 4 on page 97 and write a short dialogue between a caller and a travel expert. The caller asks about the weather in your country and the best time of year to visit.

Caller: Hello, I'm Kathy and I'm calling from New York.
Expert: Hi, Kathy.

EXTENSION

LESSON 1 Write sentences about what you are going to do next weekend. Think about Saturday and Sunday morning, afternoon and evening.

On Saturday morning I'm going to stay in bed late.

LESSON 2 Write sentences about what you like and don't like doing on holiday.

I like staying in a hotel — I don't like camping.

LESSON 3 Write sentences about people in your family using superlative adjectives.

old/young   short/tall   long/short hair   fair/dark hair

My grandfather is the oldest person in the family. I am the youngest.

LESSON 4 Look at the questions you wrote in exercise 5 on page 97. Find out the travel information and write the answers to your questions. Use the answers in exercise 2 to help you.

YOUR CHOICE!

WHAT ANIMAL AM I?

- Work in a small group.
- Each student writes down the name of a favourite animal and the answers to these questions:

  What do you look like?
  Where do you live?
  What do you eat?
  What can you do?

- One student reads out the answers to the questions but doesn't say the animal's name. The first student to guess the animal then reads out his/her answers.

WORLD RECORDS QUIZ

- Work in a small group and think about world records in these categories: people, sport, geography, history, animals, transport, films, music.
- Find out one superlative fact for each category, for example:

  the biggest   the coldest   the most expensive
  the fastest   the highest   the hottest   the longest
  the oldest   the smallest   the tallest

- Work together to write questions for a *World Records Quiz*. Ask other students to do your quiz.

What do families around the world eat?

Photographer Peter Menzel travels across continents and compares a week's food in different countries.

The Natomo Family, Kouakourou, Mali

Pama Kondo, 35, (second from the left at the back) and Fatoumata Toure, 33, (on the right at the back) and their husband Soumana Natomo, 46, (sitting between them) live in West Africa. Soumana's two wives live in two different houses, but share the housework. Their nine children also help prepare the grain, which is the largest part of the family's food. The family eat meals together outside Pama's house. Breakfast is porridge, lunch is a vegetable stew (sometimes with fish), and dinner is *tô* (a kind of cake) and soup. Their weekly food includes 50kg of grain and 20kg of rice.

The Revis Family, North Carolina, USA

Rosemary Revis, 40, and Ron Revis, 39, have two sons from Rosemary's first marriage: Brandon, 16, (on the left) and Tyrone, 14. Rosemary has a very busy American lifestyle; working in an office and looking after her family. But she finds it easy to put on weight. So does Tyrone, who eats a lot of snacks in front of the TV. When Rosemary and Tyrone joined a gym and tried to lose weight Ron and Brandon came too. The family enjoyed the gym and spent a lot of time there. But then there was less time for home-cooked meals and they ate more fast food. Now they have exercise machines at home, and their diet includes more fresh vegetables and less fast food.

The Ukita Family, north-west Tokyo, Japan

Kazuo, 53, lives with his wife Sayo, 51, and children Mio, 17, and Maya, 14, in the suburbs of Tokyo. Kazuo works in a book warehouse and Sayo looks after the children. Kazuo has soup or fish with rice for breakfast and leaves for work at 7am. Sayo and the children eat breakfast a little later. The Ukitas eat a lot of meat and fish and ten eggs a week. They also eat a lot of rice (5kg a week) but no potatoes. Before Mio started university, the family ate dinner together every day, but now this doesn't happen as often.

READING

1 🔘 3.16 Read the texts about food around the world and match them with the photos.

2 Answer the questions.

1 Which families have two children?
2 Who has two wives?
3 Which husband has breakfast alone?
4 Which family eats outside?
5 Which husband and wife are the oldest?
6 Who has a brother called Tyrone?
7 Which family eats the most rice?
8 Who has soup for breakfast?
9 Which family eats soup for dinner?
10 Which family eats fast food?

3 VOCABULARY

Match the words with their definitions.

1 largest
2 porridge
3 stew
4 diet
5 fast food

a food that a person usually eats
b food like hamburgers and pizza
c hot food made from grain and water or milk
d biggest
e meal cooked slowly in water, usually with vegetables and meat or fish

4 SPEAKING

Use the photos and texts to compare the three families and their food.

- Which things in the photos are the same and which things are different?
- Which is the biggest family?
- Which family is trying to lose weight?
- In which family do the children help with the food?
- In your opinion, which family eats the healthiest food?
- Which family's food do you like best?

5 MINI-PROJECT
Food File

Work with another student and write a comparison between the kind of food families eat in your country and in the three countries in the text. Use these questions to help you.

- What do you and your family eat in a week?
- When and where do you have breakfast, lunch and dinner?
- Who buys and cooks the food?
- Do you eat a lot of frozen food or fast food?

Read your work carefully and correct any mistakes. Show your *Food File* to other students.

In our country we usually have porridge for breakfast like the Natomo family in Mali. But we don't eat outside — we have breakfast in the kitchen.

1 I'd like a cold drink

Making and accepting/declining offers
some and *any*
Countable/Uncountable nouns
I'd like … Would you like …?

1 OPENER

Which of these can you see in the photo of the kitchen?

apples   bananas   a cooker   a cup   a dishwasher
a fridge   a fork   a glass   a knife   oranges   a plate
a sandwich   a spoon   a table   a washing machine

2 READING

3.17   Read the dialogue. What does Ruby think is a good idea?

PIERRE   Hiya – wow, I'm really thirsty!

DIANA   Would you like some tea?

PIERRE   No, thanks – I'd like a cold drink.

DIANA   There's some apple juice in the fridge. And there's some milk.

PIERRE   Apple juice is fine. Are there any bananas?

DIANA   Sorry, no, there aren't. Would you like a sandwich?

PIERRE   Yes, please.

DIANA   Help yourself. Now let's talk about the barbecue party. I'm going to buy some paper plates and plastic glasses.

RUBY   What about food? What are we going to cook?

PIERRE   Well, everyone likes hamburgers and sausages.

RUBY   I don't – I don't want any meat.

PIERRE   What do you mean? You ate some meat last night.

RUBY   Well, today I'm vegetarian.

PIERRE   You're crazy!

DIANA   OK, Ruby, let's make some vegetable kebabs.

RUBY   Mmm – good idea!

3 AFTER READING

Answer the questions.

1   Does Pierre want a cup of tea?
2   Would he like some fruit juice?
3   Does he want a banana?
4   Does Diana offer him a sandwich?
5   What is Diana going to buy?
6   Does Ruby like sausages now?
7   Why doesn't she eat any meat now?
8   What does Diana suggest they make?

Your response   What's your idea of good party food?

4 VOCABULARY

Complete the chart with these words.

Word Bank Food and drink
banana   cheese   chip   coffee   egg   fruit   meat mushroom   tea   tomato   vegetable   water

Countable		Uncountable
Singular	Plural	
a banana	*bananas*	*cheese*

5 SPEAKING

Student A: Cover the photo of the kitchen.

Student B: Ask questions about these things.

> books   chairs   cheese   magazines   meat
> milk   vegetables

Now change over.

Student B: Cover the photo of the kitchen.

Student A: Ask questions about these things.

> animals   bread   eggs   flowers   fruit   pens   water

> Is/Are there any …
> in the photo?

> Yes, there
> is/are.

> No, there
> isn't/aren't.

> **Extension**   Choose a photo in this book and show it to another student. Then take the book away and ask your partner questions about the photo.

6 VOCABULARY

3.18   Match the words with the pictures. Then listen and check.

> **Word Bank** Food
>
> chocolate cake   fruit salad   hamburgers   ice cream
> kebabs   potatoes   sausages   tomato salad

7 LISTENING

3.19   Listen to the conversation and number these sentences in the right order.

A   Yes, please.

B   And would you like some sausages?

C   What would you like to eat?

D   No, thank you. I don't want any sausages.

E   Would you like some potatoes?

F   I'd like a hamburger and some tomato salad, please.

8 PRONUNCIATION

3.20   Listen and repeat.

/eɪ/ plate	/æ/ thanks	/ɑ:/ glass
make	apple	barbecue
paper	salad	banana

Write these words in the correct column. Then listen and check.

> cake   carrot   crazy   hamburger   last
> party   potato   sandwich   tomato

9 SPEAKING

Look at the food in exercise 6 and choose three things you'd like to eat. Then act out a conversation in pairs. Use the phrases in the box to help you.

Making offers	**Accepting**
What would you like to eat?	I'd like a/some …
Would you like a/some …?	Yes, please.

Declining
No, thanks/thank you.
I don't want a/any …

10 WRITING

Write a conversation between two people at a party. A offers B some food, but doesn't know that B is vegetarian.

A   *What would you like to eat?*

B   *I'd like …*

LANGUAGE WORKOUT

Complete.

some
There's **some** apple juice in the fridge.
You ate _____ meat last night.
Let's make _____ kebabs.

We use *some* in affirmative sentences with plural nouns and uncountable nouns *like bread* and *milk*.
We also use *some* in questions making offers:
Would you like **some** tea?

any
Are there **any** bananas?
I don't want _____ meat.

We use *any* in neutral questions and negative sentences.

Countable nouns		Uncountable nouns
Singular	**Plural**	✗bread milk✗
an apple	apples	
a sandwich	sandwiches	

▶**Answers and Practice**
Language File page 121

I haven't got a games console

Talking about money and prices
Talking about possessions
have got
Question: How much … ?

Where does all the money go?

A recent survey shows that, on average, British teenagers cost their parents £9,000 a year.

We asked two teenagers three questions:

● *How much money do you get a week?* ● *What do you spend your money on?*

● *How much do you think parents spend on a teenager in a year?*

Emil Ahmed, 15

I get £30 a week allowance from my parents. I normally spend it going out with my friends. We go to the cinema, ice-skating, things like that. I think I get quite a lot compared with my friends.

I've got one contract phone and one pay-as-you-go phone. My parents pay for the contract one and I pay for the other. I find it easier to have one phone for friends and one phone for the family. I haven't got a games console, so I use my brother's. I pay for the games myself.

How much do parents spend on teenagers? Around £4,500 a year – but I'm not too sure about that.

Freya Brightwater, 13

I get about the same amount of pocket money as most of my friends – £5 a week. But I also help my mum, who cleans some cottages near us, and I get paid £6 an hour for that.

I've got a mobile phone. It's really old – I bought it two years ago and it only cost £14. I can't get a new one at the moment because I haven't got much money in my bank account. I've got an iPod® and a Nintendo DS, which I bought myself with birthday money. I never shop at expensive places. I see things that cost £150 and think: 'Why do you pay so much for one thing?'

How much do parents spend a year on teenagers? Some people have loads of money – so maybe £7,500.

1 OPENER

Look at the photos. Guess: Which teenager gets the most money every week?

2 READING

🔘 3.21 Read the article and compare yourself with Emil and Freya.

3 AFTER READING

Match the questions with the answers. There is one wrong answer.

1 Who has got two phones?
2 Has Emil got a games console?
3 Who hasn't got a new phone?
4 Who has got a job?
5 Have both Emil and Freya got phones?
6 Who thinks teenagers cost half what they really cost?
7 Has Freya got an iPod®?

a Freya.
b Yes, she has.
c Yes, they have.
d Emil does.
e Yes, he has.
f Emil has.
g No, he hasn't.
h Freya has.

Your response How much do you think teenagers cost their parents in your country?

4 LISTENING

🔘 3.22 Emily and Jake go shopping. Listen and match the things with the prices.

> computer game   DVD   Blu-ray disc
> CD   poster   magazine

£12.75   99p   £15.99   £22.50   £1.25   £16

Now ask and answer.

> How much is the computer game?

> It's twenty-two fifty.

5 PRONUNCIATION

🔘 3.23 Listen and repeat.

/f/   /v/   /w/
We love watching
movies – we've got
twenty-five DVDs with
our fifty-one favourite films!

6 LISTENING

🔘 3.24 Listen and complete the chart.

has got ✓   hasn't got ✗

	Teresa	Pierre	Katya	Adam
brother				
sister				
camera phone				
pet				
skateboard				
hobby				

Now ask and answer.

> Has Teresa got a camera phone?

> Yes, she has.

> Who's got a camera phone?

> Teresa and Adam have.

> **Extension** Write sentences about the characters.
> *Teresa hasn't got any brothers or sisters. Pierre, Katya and Adam have all got sisters.*

7 SPEAKING

Ask questions about other students and note down the answers. Ask about:

family   possessions   hobbies

> Has he got any brothers or sisters?

> Yes, he has. He's got one sister.

> Has she got a hobby?

> Yes, she has. She loves riding.

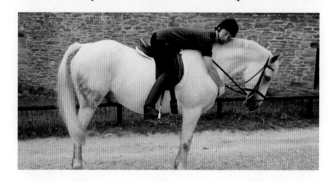

> **Extension** Do a class survey.
> What is the most popular hobby in the class?
> Who has got most hobbies?

8 WRITING

Use your notes from exercise 7 and write short descriptions of three students. Don't write their names!

She's got three brothers, but she hasn't got any sisters.

Now give your descriptions to another student. Can your partner guess all the names?

LANGUAGE WORKOUT

Complete.

have got

Affirmative	**Contractions**
I/you/we/they **have got**	I/you/we/they **'ve** _____
he/she/it **has got**	he/she/it **'s** _____

Negative

I/you/we/they _____ **not got**	I/you/we/they **haven't** _____
he/she/it **has** _____ **got**	he/she it _____ **got**

Questions	**Short answers**
Has he **got** a games console?	Yes, he **has**.
	No, he **hasn't**.
_____ they **got** phones?	Yes, they **have**.
	No, they _____.
Who _____ **got** a job?	I _____.

We use *have got* like *have* to talk about possessions. There is no continuous form.

▶**Answers and Practice**
Language File page 121

8

HOME FROM HOME

3 It's different, isn't it?

Asking for agreement
Question tags with *be*

A Child from Everywhere

In the United Kingdom, there are children and teenagers from 185 countries – almost every country in the world.

Inza, 15, from Ivory Coast
When my parents told me 'Inza, you're going to go to England', I was so excited. I thought England was paradise. But it's just a little country, it's a normal country, like every country in the world. In Africa when you see anyone walking around, you just say hello. But in England when you say hello, they don't say hello back. I miss the free life in Africa. There I can go out at six o'clock in the morning and I can come back at one o'clock at night. Safe, safe, nothing's going to happen to me. But here it's different, isn't it?

Luis, 15, from Peru
At the beginning I didn't want to come here. I wanted to stay in Peru with my friends. When I was in Peru, I was confident about going out and hanging around in town and stuff. But I'm not as confident about doing those things in England. I don't know why, but I feel like I'm not part of England. My mother is a doctor and I would like to study medicine and then go back and work in my country.

Amna, 15, from Bahrain I feel at home here. Here, people really understand. I guess because London is filled with people from all sorts of places. Just walking down the street I see different people, and hear different languages. I even hear Arabic a lot. It makes me feel that I'm still connected with my culture, and at the same time I'm learning about other cultures.

Fidan, 12, from Azerbaijan
When I tell people that I'm from Azerbaijan, they ask 'Where's that?' I'm really happy to be Azeri because Azeri culture is a rich culture. Our language is good, our music's good – it's got more rhythm than English music – and our food's delicious. But I only like Azerbaijan for holidays. I really like living in England because I have more friends here.

1 OPENER

Look at the photos. Guess: How are the people feeling?

2 READING

🔊 3.25 Read the article. Which countries are the people from? Where are the four countries?

3 AFTER READING

True, false, or no information?

1 Inza thinks some things about life in Africa are better than in England.
2 At first Luis was excited about living in England.
3 Only Luis tells us what he wants to study.
4 Amna enjoys living in a country where there are lots of different nationalities.
5 Amna likes learning languages.
6 Fidan likes Azeri music more than English music.
7 Fidan has more friends in Azerbaijan than in England.
8 All four like life in the UK more than life in the country they came from.

Your response Would you like to live in another country? Why/Why not? If yes, which country?

4 LISTENING

🔘 3.26 Listen to the conversation at the barbecue. Then listen again and answer the questions.

1 Who is Katya talking to?
2 Who wants some ice cream?
3 Which two are getting on well?
4 Who is sad?
5 Who is going to stay with Katya?
6 Who drops her glass?

5 PRONUNCIATION

🔘 3.27 Listen and complete the sentences with these question tags.

> isn't she? isn't he? isn't it? aren't I?
> aren't we? aren't you? aren't they?

1 We're enjoying the barbecue, _____?
2 It's hot, _____?
3 They're getting on well, _____?
4 Mr Campbell is cooking sausages, _____?
5 Ruby is happy, _____?
6 You're Katya, _____?
7 I *am* silly, _____?

Now listen again and repeat the sentences.

6 READING

Do the quiz. You can find all the answers in this book!

New Inspiration 1 **Quiz**

1 What does Mika do?
2 Where are California and Colorado?
3 Which is the most dangerous animal in the world?
4 What's the capital of Australia?
5 How old is the Taj Mahal?
6 What does Lewis Hamilton do?
7 Where are Linkin Park from?
8 How old is the Royal Pavilion in Brighton?
9 Is the world getting hotter or colder?
10 Who is the book *Dracula* by?

Now check your answers with other students.

> What does Mika do?

> He's a ..., isn't he?

> **Extension** Write five more quiz questions. Ask two other students to do your quiz.

7 WRITING

Write a paragraph about a character in *New Inspiration 1*. Describe something that he/she did during the exchange visit.

Now read out your paragraph, but don't say the name. Can the other students guess who it is?

LANGUAGE WORKOUT

Complete.

Question tags with *be*

It's a great party, **isn't it**?   You're Teresa, _____n't you?
She's sad, _____n't she?   They're having fun, _____n't they?

BUT I'm late, **aren't I**?

▶**Answers and Practice**
Language File page 121

107

4 Integrated Skills
Invitations and thanks

1 OPENER

Look at the cards, messages and emails. What are they about?

2 READING

🔘 3.28 Match the invitations 1–4 with the replies A–D. Then listen and check.

Invitations

1

INVITATION

❋ ❋ ❋

The Campbell family invite
all the NFI Exchange Students
to a Barbecue Party to celebrate the end of the visit.

Sunday 24th July   2–6pm

❋ ❋ ❋

8 Hill Street, Lewes   RSVP Tel 837921

2

| Ruby | 10:04 |

Hi everyone!
Come to our party!
It's in Adam's room and starts after the barbecue.
Bring some good music and dance the night away!
Be there or be square!
Ruby and Adam

3

File   Edit   View   Favorites   Tools   Help   Links »

To: Mr Ward and the Brighton High School students

Thank you very much for giving Jake such a good time. He really enjoyed himself and also learned a lot about life in Britain.

We are looking forward to Adam's visit to Washington. We hope that he can come to a welcome lunch at our school when he arrives.

With best wishes

Bart Hellyer

School Principal

4

Dear Diana

There's a buffet lunch at the school on Monday after the NFI students leave. The Head wants to thank the parents for all their hard work during the exchange.

I hope you and your family can come. Please let me know.

David Ward

Replies

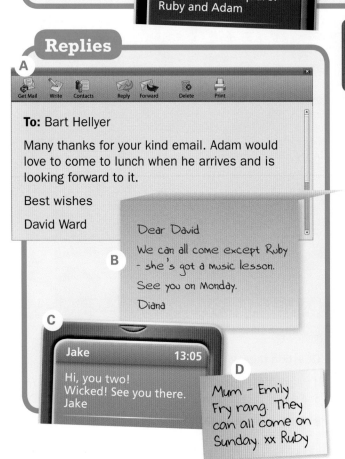

A

Get Mail   Write   Contacts   Reply   Forward   Delete   Print

To: Bart Hellyer

Many thanks for your kind email. Adam would love to come to lunch when he arrives and is looking forward to it.

Best wishes

David Ward

B

Dear David

We can all come except Ruby – she's got a music lesson.

See you on Monday.

Diana

C

| Jake | 13:05 |

Hi, you two!
Wicked! See you there.
Jake

D

Mum – Emily Fry rang. They can all come on Sunday. xx Ruby

Katya's thank-you letter

Pushkin Prospekt, 4
Moscow
Russia
26th July

Dear Mr and Mrs Fry,

Thank you very much for looking after me so well. I really enjoyed staying with you in Brighton.

We had an easy journey home and it's nice to see my family again. But I miss Brighton!

The three things I miss most are:

Emily – because she was nice and friendly to me – like a sister.

Your food – I learnt a lot about English cooking. It was wonderful.

All the Brighton High School students – they were great fun, especially Adam!

I hope that you are both well. My parents send their best wishes and we're all looking forward to Emily's visit.

With best wishes,

Katya

3 Read Katya's thank-you letter and complete.

1 The thank-you letter is from Katya to _____.
2 Katya's address is _____.
3 The date of the letter is _____.
4 The _____ paragraph is about her journey home.
5 There are _____ things which Katya misses.
6 _____ parents send their _____.
7 Katya's family are looking forward to _____.
8 The letter ends: With _____, Katya.

4 LISTENING

🔘 3.29 Listen to the phone calls and choose the correct words.

Call 1

Adam wants Emily to go to the Zero Club with him tomorrow/tonight. There's a new DJ at the club who plays terrible/wicked music. Emily makes an excuse about lots of homework and says no/yes.

Call 2

Pierre rings Ruby from Brighton/Geneva and invites her to stay with his family/school. Ruby accepts/says no and goes to talk to her mother.

Call 3

Emily tells her friend Lisa about Adam and then invites her to go to the cinema/Zero Club. Lisa accepts and they are going to meet at seven/eight o'clock.

5 SPEAKING

Look at the invitations and replies in exercise 2 and the notes in exercise 4 again. Then role play three phone calls between two friends. You can use the phrases in the box.

1 an invitation to a party
2 an invitation to the theatre
3 an invitation to dinner

A   B

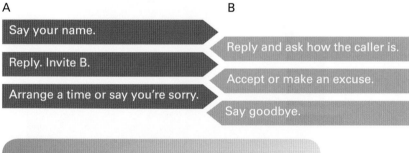

Say your name.

Reply and ask how the caller is.

Reply. Invite B.

Accept or make an excuse.

Arrange a time or say you're sorry.

Say goodbye.

Inviting	Accepting
Would you like to …?	Yes, please. I'd love to.
Do you want to …?	Yes, of course. That's great.

Declining/Making an excuse
No, thanks/thank you.
I'm not sure.
I'm sorry, I can't. I'm busy.

6 WRITING

Look at the thank-you letter in exercise 2. Write a thank-you letter from Jake to Mr Ward.

Open the letter.
Paragraph 1 Say thank you.
Paragraph 2 Write about your journey home.
Paragraph 3 Write about three things you miss.
Paragraph 4 Write about your parents and Adam's arrival.
Close the letter.

LEARNER INDEPENDENCE

7 This is the last unit of the book. What are you going to do about your English in the holidays? Order these suggestions 1–8.

1 Look back through this book and the workbook again.
2 Learn a section of my vocabulary notebook every day.
3 Listen to songs in English (and find the words on the Web).
4 Find English at home – on food packets, on CDs, on TV, and in newspapers and magazines.
5 Look up new words in an English-English dictionary.
6 Write to an epal in English.
7 Read easy books in English.
8 Practise the sketches from Inspiration *Extra!* with a friend.

8 Add these sections to your vocabulary notebook.

Things in the kitchen
Food and drink (add to your list from Unit 3)
Favourite words

9 🔘 3.30 **Phrasebook:** Find these useful expressions in Unit 8. Then listen and repeat.

Hiya.
I'm really thirsty.
No, thanks.
Yes, please.
You're crazy.
Come to our party!
Please let me know.
Wicked!
See you there.

Now complete these three exchanges with your own words.

A …
B No, thanks.

A …
B You're crazy!

A …
B Wicked!

Inspiration EXTRA!

PROJECT *Home and Away*

1 There are always special things – good and bad – which make countries different from each other. Work in a group and choose a foreign country which you are interested in.

2 Research: Use the Internet and your library to make notes about positive and negative aspects of the country you chose. Use these headings:

People	friendly, helpful, busy, open, serious?
Food and drink	special dishes and drinks?
Weather	hot/cold, rainy/dry, summer/winter?
Languages	how many?
Culture	music, dancing, theatre, painting?
Anything else?	something unusual?

3 Now make notes about your own country under the same headings.

4 Work together and use your notes to decide on the three best things and two worst things in your country (Home) and the foreign country (Away).

5 Write about the best and worst things in both countries. Read your work carefully and correct any mistakes. Find pictures of the countries from magazines or online for your project. Show your work to the other groups.

HOME Scotland

BEST

Friendly people who like meeting visitors.

Wonderful Scottish dancing.

At important events men wear skirts called 'kilts'.

WORST

It rains, and it rains and it rains.

The Scottish accent – it's hard to understand.

AWAY Sweden

BEST

Hot summers with blue skies and cold snowy winters.

Everyone speaks English!

The countryside – beautiful lakes and rivers.

WORST

Food and drink are very expensive.

The days are very short in winter.

Game *Word Maze*

- Work in pairs to move from *FRUIT* to *HAPPY*.

- Move from line to line by word association – find a word in the next line which goes with your word.

- The first pair to get to *HAPPY* is the winner.

FRUIT				
cup	spoon	fork	glass	juice
cook	make	drink	offer	suggest
sandwich	eat	bread	flowers	salad
party food	DVD	CD	mobile phone	camera
hobby	pet	possession	invitation	family
thank-you letter	skateboard	computer game	girlfriend	washing machine
sausage	vegetarian	barbecue	ice cream	present
buffet	excuse	birthday	exchange	cooking
HAPPY				

REVISION

LESSON 1 Look at the photo of the kitchen on page 102. Write questions and answers about the things in the kitchen.

Is/Are there any ...?
Yes, there is/are. No, there isn't/aren't.

LESSON 2 Look at the chart in exercise 6 on page 105 and write sentences about the characters.

Teresa hasn't got any brothers or sisters.

LESSON 3 Look at exercise 5 on page 107 and write sentences about what the people are doing using question tags.

Pierre and Ruby are sitting together, aren't they?

LESSON 4 Look at the role play in exercise 5 on page 109. Write out one of the conversations.

A   Hi Anna, it's Maria.

EXTENSION

LESSON 1 Look at the conversation in exercise 7 on page 103. Write a conversation between two people at a party. A offers B some food but B always says no in a different way. (B doesn't want to say he/she had a meal before the party).

A Would you like some tomato salad?
B No, thank you. I don't like tomatoes.

LESSON 2 Look at exercise 7 on page 105 and write short descriptions of three members of your family.

My father has got a great hobby – flying.

LESSON 3 Look at exercise 6 on page 107. Write your own five-question General Knowledge Quiz. Ask three other students to do your quiz.

LESSON 4 Look at exercise 6 on page 109. Write Pierre's thank-you letter to Diana and Steven Campbell.

Dear Mr and Mrs Campbell,
Thank you ...

YOUR CHOICE!

LOOKING BACK AND LOOKING FORWARD

- Work in a small group.
- Have a discussion about your English lessons and *New Inspiration 1*. Talk about:
  – three things you like about the lessons and the book.
  – something you want to change.
  – something you want to do in your English lessons next year.
- Now write a note for your teacher giving your opinions.

TOUCH SOMETHING

- Work in a small group. Look around at all the things in the classroom, for example, furniture, equipment, clothes. Think about their colour, shape, size, temperature and how they feel.
- Take turns to tell the rest of the group what to touch.

  Touch something red.
  Touch something round.
  Touch something that feels soft.
- The student who touches the object first is the winner.

REVIEW

1 Read and complete. For each number 1–12, choose word A, B or C.

FOOTBALL HERO

People everywhere love ___1___ football – also called soccer – and it's the ___2___ sport in the world. But who is the ___3___ footballer of all time? Many people agree that the ___4___ player in the world is Edson Arantes do Nascimento, better known as Pele.

Born in 1940, Pele is from the south-east of Brazil. Life was very difficult when he was a child ___5___ his family didn't have ___6___ money. Like lots of other Brazilian boys, he started playing football in the street, often with a ball made of ___7___ old socks. But at the age of 16 he started playing for Brazil and he soon became the ___8___ man in the country. He helped Brazil to win the World Cup in 1958, 1962 and 1970.

Pele played his last games with the New York Cosmos, and he made soccer a ___9___ sport in the USA. The 'beautiful game' is in his family. ___10___ got six children, and his son Edinho was a goalkeeper for Santos, Pele's Brazilian club.

In 1999, the National Olympic® Committee named Pele 'Sportsman of the Century'. He knows he is a football hero. 'Pele ___11___ die. But Edson is an ordinary person who ___12___ die one day, and people forget that.'

1	A	play	B	playing	C	are playing
2	A	popular	B	more popular	C	most popular
3	A	best	B	better	C	good
4	A	biggest	B	greatest	C	highest
5	A	then	B	why	C	because
6	A	some	B	any	C	lots
7	A	some	B	any	C	lots
8	A	famous	B	more famous	C	most famous
9	A	the popular	B	more popular	C	most popular
10	A	He is	B	He's	C	He had
11	A	going to	B	isn't going	C	isn't going to
12	A	is going	B	is going to	C	are going to

2 Ask and answer.

Pierre/phone home ✓
A Is Pierre going to phone home?
B Yes, he is.

1 Ruby and Adam/cook dinner ✗
2 Emily/play the saxophone ✗
3 Adam/do his homework ✓
4 Katya and Teresa/buy some presents ✓
5 Pierre/paint a picture ✗
6 Jake/wear new trainers ✓

Now write sentences.

Pierre is going to phone home.

3 Match the questions with the answers and write sentences.

1 Why is Adam sitting at his computer?
2 Why are Teresa and Emily standing outside the cinema?
3 Why is Katya in a shoe shop?
4 Why is Diana buying a ticket?
5 Why are Pierre and Jake going to the sports centre?

a Because she's going to buy some trainers.
b Because they're going to play tennis.
c Because he's going to send an email.
d Because they're going to see a film.
e Because she's going to catch a train.

Adam is sitting at his computer because …

4 Write sentences using the gerund.

Emily/love/go to the cinema
Emily loves going to the cinema.

1 Katya/like/draw horses
2 Adam and Ruby/hate/eat garlic
3 Emily/enjoy/play the guitar
4 I/not mind/swim in cold water
5 you/like/dance?
6 we/love/go to the beach

5 Complete the sentences with the superlative form of these adjectives.

big exciting good high long old

1 I think skydiving is the _____ sport.
2 The Amazon is the _____ river in South America.
3 Russia is the _____ country in the world.
4 Mount Kilimanjaro is the _____ mountain in Africa.
5 A French woman was the _____ person in the world – she died at 122.
6 Reading books is one of the _____ ways to learn a language.

6 Choose *some* or *any*.

1 Katya is going to buy some/any apples.
2 Would you like some/any sausages?
3 There aren't some/any glasses on the table.
4 Let's make some/any hamburgers for dinner.
5 I'm not going to eat some/any potatoes.
6 Are there some/any pizzas on the menu?

7 Countable or uncountable? Complete with *a* or *some*.

1 Would you like _____ toast for breakfast?
2 I'd like _____ cup of coffee.
3 Can I have _____ milk, please?
4 She's going to make _____ tomato soup.
5 I only had _____ sandwich for lunch.
6 We're going to buy _____ meat for the kebabs.
7 Do you want _____ glass of fruit juice?
8 Let's listen to _____ music.

8 Ask and answer.

A How much is the bag?
B It's seventeen fifty.

9 Put the words in the right order to make sentences.

1 got she red eyes has and hair green .
2 haven't lot I a money got of .
3 any or sisters got you brothers have ?
4 some has she jeans new got .
5 game got who the computer has best ?
6 answers we all right the got have !

10 Complete with question tags.

1 Teresa is Spanish, _____?
2 Pierre is thirsty, _____?
3 Katya and Emily are friends, _____?
4 Emily's surname is Fry, _____?
5 We're good at English, _____?
6 You're having fun, _____?

VOCABULARY

11 Complete with ten of these words.

> camel fridge hobby hospital invitation
> kill knitting medicine pet prize
> vegetarian washing machine

1 He went to the _____ because he felt very ill.
2 It's a good idea to keep milk in the _____.
3 Someone who doesn't eat meat is a _____.
4 The _____ is often called 'the ship of the desert'.
5 Hippos are really dangerous – they _____ lots of
   people.
6 A dog is the most popular _____ in Britain.
7 You can ask your doctor for some _____.
8 You can wash your clothes in a _____.
9 Skateboarding is the favourite _____ of lots of
   teenagers.
10 Ruby made her pullover – she likes _____.

12 Match these words with their definitions.

> chess dishwasher giraffe kitchen
> knife malaria plate slow

1 opposite of *fast*
2 mosquitoes carry this disease
3 the tallest animal in the world
4 you cut things with this
5 you wash plates and cups in this
6 room where you prepare food
7 you put food on this
8 board game with black and white pieces

13 Match the verbs in list A with the words and phrases
in list B.

	A	B
1	buy	an ambulance
2	die	how to surf
3	call	of malaria
4	get on	money
5	learn	well
6	look	a ticket
7	spend	worried

LEARNER INDEPENDENCE
SELF ASSESSMENT

Look back at Lessons 1–3 in Units 7 and 8.

How good are you at …?	✓Fine	? Not sure
1 Talking about future plans and intentions Workbook p78 exercises 1–3	☐	☐
2 Asking for and giving reasons Workbook p79 exercise 4	☐	☐
3 Talking about likes and dislikes Workbook pp80–81 exercises 1–5	☐	☐
4 Making comparisons Workbook pp82–83 exercises 1–3	☐	☐
5 Making and accepting/declining offers Workbook p90 exercise 1	☐	☐
6 Talking about money and prices Workbook p93 exercise 5	☐	☐
7 Talking about possessions Workbook pp92–93 exercises 1, 2 and 4	☐	☐
8 Asking for agreement Workbook pp94–95 exercises 2 and 3	☐	☐

**Not sure? Have a look at Language File pages 120–121
and do the Workbook exercise(s) again.**

Now write an example for 1–8

1 Adam is going to play basketball.

LANGUAGE FILE

Present simple: *be* and personal pronouns

WELCOME!

Affirmative	
Full forms	**Contractions**
I am	I'm
you are	you're
he is	he's
she is	she's
it is	it's
we are	we're
they are	they're
Negative	
I am not	I'm not
you are not	you aren't
he is not	he isn't
she is not	she isn't
it is not	it isn't
we are not	we aren't
they are not	they aren't
Questions	**Short answers**
am I?	Yes, you are./No, you aren't.
are you?	Yes, I am./No, I'm not.
is he?	Yes, he is./No, he isn't.
is she?	Yes, she is./No, she isn't.
is it?	Yes, it is./No, it isn't.
are we?	Yes, we are./No, we aren't.
are they?	Yes, they are./No, they aren't.

- In questions with the verb *be*, the verb comes before the subject:
  Are you English?
  Where is Adam from?
- We make the negative by adding *not*.
- We use the full form in affirmative short answers and the contraction in negative short answers:
  Yes, she is.   No, she isn't.

PRACTICE: Present simple *be*

1 Complete with the correct form of *be*.

1 Her name *is* Teresa and she _____ from Spain.
2 Emily and Adam _____ at school in Brighton.
3 We _____ pleased to be here.
4 My name _____ David Ward and I _____ a teacher.
5 His name _____ Pierre. He _____ from Switzerland.
6 Emily and Adam _____ English.

2 Complete the questions and answers.

1 _____ Emily and Adam American? No, they _____.
2 _____ David Ward a student? No, he _____.
3 _____ you from the USA? No, I _____.
4 _____ you English? No, we _____.
5 _____ Katya from Brighton? No, she _____.

---

this/that and *these/those*

UNIT 1 LESSONS 1 AND 2

Singular		Plural
this		these
that		those

- We use *this/these* to talk about things **here**:
  This is my favourite bag.   What's this in English?
  These are copies of the programme.
- We use *that/those* to talk about things **over there**:
  That's a great bag.   That's my rucksack over there.
  Look at all those bicycles!

PRACTICE: *this/that* and *these/those*

3 Choose *these* or *those*.

1 Look in this bag! These/Those are my new DVDs.
2 Are these/those your friends over there?
3 Who are these/those people in that picture?
4 Here, these/those are photos of my family.
5 These/Those cities are all in Europe: Brussels, Geneva, Madrid.
6 These/Those buildings in that street are very old.

Indefinite article: *a/an* + singular nouns

UNIT 1 LESSON 1

- We use *a* before singular nouns beginning with **consonants** or with *u* /juː/:
  a bag   a passport   a university
- We use *an* before singular nouns beginning with **vowels**, including *u* /ʌ/, and silent *h*:
  an alarm clock   an ID card   an MP3 /em piː θriː/ player
  an umbrella   an hour
- We use the indefinite article:
a when the noun is mentioned for the first time:
  That's a great bag.   Here's a picture of Geneva.
b with nouns for jobs and occupations:
  He's a teacher.   She's a student.
c with some numbers and expressions of quantity:
  a hundred   a thousand   a lot   a few

Plural nouns

UNIT 1 LESSON 2

- **Spelling**
  We add *s* to most nouns to make the plural:
  bicycles   maps   visitors   years
- We add *es* to nouns ending in *ss*, *ch*, *sh*, *x*, and to some nouns ending in *o*:
  addresses   watches   wishes   boxes   tomatoes
- For nouns ending in a consonant + *y*, we change the *y* to *i* and add *es*:
  city – cities   copy – copies   party – parties
  BUT *boy – boys   day – days*
- **Irregular plurals:**
  *person – **people**   man – **men**   woman – **women***
  *child – **children***

Prepositions of place

UNIT 1 LESSON 2

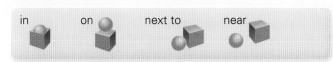

- **in**

    What's in your bag?
    We're in the centre of the city.
    Delhi is in India.
    Who are the people in the photo?
    He's in the orange T-shirt.
    It's in the centre/middle of Istanbul.
    What's this in English?

- **on**

    The key is on the table.
    Where are we on the map?
    It's on page 14.
    It's on a mountain in Peru.
    There are pictures on the wall.
    She's on the left.
    He's on the right.

- **next to**

    Room 21 is next to Room 20.

- **near**

    Manchester is near Liverpool.

Personal pronouns and possessive adjectives

UNIT 1 LESSON 3

Personal pronouns	Possessive adjectives
I	me
you	your
he/she/it	his/her/its
we	our
you	your
they	their

- The personal pronoun *I* is always a capital letter.
- Possessive adjectives do not change with plural nouns:

    my friend   my friends

> **PRACTICE: Possessive adjectives**
>
> **4** Look back at exercise 2 on page 16 and complete the sentences about Katya's family with possessive adjectives.
>
> 1 Anna: '_____ brother is called Dima.'
> 2 Vera and Mikhail: 'Valentina is _____ daughter.'
> 3 Katya: 'This is my sister and _____ name is Anna.'
> 4 Mr and Mrs Petrova are called Maxim and Valentina, and _____ children are Katya, Anna and Dima.
> 5 Dima is Anna's brother and _____ T-shirt is orange.
> 6 Pierre: 'Is that _____ sister?'
>   Katya: 'No, it isn't, it's _____ mother.'

Present simple: *have*

UNIT 2 LESSON 1

> **Affirmative**
> I/you/we/they **have**
> he/she/it **has**

- We can use *have* to talk about possession:

    They have black trousers.
    He has a football.

- We can also use *have* to talk about families and to describe people:

    I have two brothers.
    He has one sister.
    She has long blonde hair.

> **PRACTICE: *have***
>
> **5** Complete with the correct form of *have*.
>
> 1 Adam _____ a sister.
> 2 Teresa _____ a bicycle.
> 3 The students _____ new books.
> 4 Emily _____ long hair.
> 5 I _____ a book called *New Inspiration*.
> 6 We _____ a good teacher.

can and *can't*

UNIT 2 LESSONS 1 AND 2

Affirmative	**Negative**
I can play the guitar.	I can't speak Spanish.
She can sing.	She can't play the piano.
Questions	**Short answers**
Can you play the sax?	Yes, I/we can.
	No, I/we can't.
Can they sing?	Yes, they can.
	No, they can't.

- We use *can* to talk about ability:

    I can sing.
    I can't find the light switch.
    What other instruments can you play?

- We also use *can* to make requests, and to ask and give/refuse permission:

    Can I open a window?
    Can I borrow your mobile?
    Yes, of course you can.
    Can I go home?
    Yes, you can./No, I'm sorry, you can't.
    Contraction: *can't* = *cannot*

- *can* is a modal auxiliary verb:

    – it does not change with *he/she/it.*
    – there is no *to* between *can* and the main verb:

    She can t̶o̶ play the guitar.

PRACTICE: *can* and *can't*

6 Write questions and answers.

Teresa/play an instrument
Can Teresa play an instrument?
No, she can't.

1 Emily/speak Spanish
2 Emily/play the sax
3 Teresa/sing
4 Emily/play the piano
5 Teresa/find the light switch
6 Emily/find the light switch

Linking words: *and, but, or*

UNIT 2 LESSON 2

- We use *and* to connect two similar ideas:
  I can play the guitar and the piano.
- We use *but* to connect two contrasting ideas:
  I can't play an instrument, but I can sing.
- We use *or* to connect alternative ideas:
  I can't speak Spanish or German.

PRACTICE: Linking words: *and, but, or*

7 Complete with *and, but, or*.

1 Can you play the guitar _____ sing at the same time?
2 I can't play the sax, _____ I can play the piano.
3 She can speak French _____ Spanish.
4 I can't see my shoes _____ my trainers.
5 They can sing in English, _____ they can't sing in German.
6 He can't speak French _____ Italian.

Imperatives

UNIT 2 LESSON 3

- We can use imperatives to give instructions, commands and advice:
  Go to Menu.
  Keep still.
  Check the microphone.
- We use *don't* before the verb to tell or advise someone **not** to do something:
  Don't move around.
  Don't sit with your back to a window.
  Don't use your mobile.
  Contraction: *don't = do not*

PRACTICE: Imperatives

8 Use the imperative to turn these requests into commands.

1 Can you please phone your parents?
2 Please don't use mobile phones in class.
3 Can you give me the number, please?
4 Can you please spell your name?
5 Please don't tell people my phone number.

Definite article: *the*

UNIT 2 LESSON 3

- We use *the* /ðə/ before nouns beginning with consonants or with *u* /juː/:
  the country   the numbers   the USA
- We use *the* /ði/ before nouns beginning with vowels, including *u* /ʌ/, and silent *h*:
  the answer   the evening   the umbrella   the hour
- We use the definite article:
a when there's only one of something:
  Dial the international code.
  The capital of Switzerland is Berne.
b when the noun has been mentioned before, or when the reference is clear:
  What's the number?
  Check the microphone.
  Answer the questions.
c before singular nouns which refer to a whole group:
  The elephant is larger than the hippo.
d before ordinal numbers and superlatives:
  the first   the largest   the most famous
e before musical instruments after *play*:
  She plays the saxophone.
f before the names of rivers, seas, oceans and some countries:
  the Nile   the Caribbean Sea   the Atlantic Ocean   the USA
  the United Kingdom
g with phrases of position:
  in the centre/middle   on the left/right
  in the north/south/east/west
h in some other phrases:
  Let's go to the cinema.
  I like listening to the radio.

Zero article

- We do **not** use the article:
a before languages and subjects:
  I like French and history.
b before the names of most countries, towns and streets:
  Spain   Brighton   Park Road
c in some phrases:
  They're at school.
  I stayed in bed.
  He works at night.
  Let's have breakfast.

Present simple

UNIT 3 LESSONS 1 AND 2, UNIT 5 LESSON 1

Affirmative	Negative
I like	I **don't** like
you like	you **don't** like
he/she/it like**s**	he/she/it **doesn't** like
we like	we **don't** like
they like	they **don't** like
Questions	**Short answers**
Do you/they like …?	Yes, I/we/they **do**.
	No, I/we/they **don't**.
Does he/she/it like …?	Yes, he/she/it **does**.
	No, he/she/it **doesn't**.

- We use the present simple to describe states, routines, timetables and regular activities:
  We live in a flat.
  Every day she gets up at six.
  He has geography on Thursday.
  At midday I start cooking lunch.
  In the afternoon, they read and sunbathe.
  She sits outside and looks at the stars.

- We also use the present simple to talk about what people do in their jobs and occupations:

  What does he do? (= What's his job?)
  He's a pilot. He flies planes to South-east Asia.
- The verb does not change in the present simple affirmative except after *he, she, it*:

  he lives   she lives   it lives
- Present simple negative: subject + *do/does not* + verb:

  I really don't like octopus.
  We don't have a garden.
  Contractions: *don't* = do not   *doesn't* = does not
- Present simple questions: *do/does* + subject + verb:

  When do you have dinner?
  Does she study in the evening?
  In *does* questions, the main verb does not end in *s*:
  What time does she gets up?

PRACTICE: Present simple

9 Write sentences using the present simple.

Pierre/like/the cottage
Pierre likes the cottage.

1	Ruby/like/Pierre	5	you/not speak/Chinese
2	he/not have/a sister	6	Diana/love/fish
3	we/love/music	7	I/not want/eggs for breakfast
4	they/not like/octopus	8	sometimes Ruby/hate/Adam

10 Complete the questions and answer them.

1 _____ students at your school pay for books and meals?
2 _____ your school have a football team?
3 _____ you like football?
4 _____ students at your school play tennis?
5 _____ your school have a break in the morning?
6 _____ you have music lessons at your school?

Prepositions of time

UNIT 3 LESSON 2

- We use *at* for specific times:

  at four o'clock   at noon   at midnight
  and in some fixed phrases:
  at night   at the weekend
- We use *in* for periods of time during the day (except *night*), months and years:

  in the morning/afternoon/evening   in July   in 1983
- We use *on* for days and dates:

  on Monday/Tuesday (morning)   on 27 July
- We use *from … to* for the beginning and end of a period of time:

  from half past three to quarter past four

Adverbs of frequency

UNIT 3 LESSON 3

always   usually   often   sometimes   never
100% – – – – – – – – – – – – – – – – – 0%

- The adverb goes after the verb *be*:

  It is always busy.   Pronoun + be + adverb
  The adverb goes before other verbs:
  I often go there.   Pronoun + adverb + verb

PRACTICE: Adverbs of frequency

11 Rewrite these sentences with the adverb in the correct position.

1 Emily goes to the gym at the weekend. (sometimes)
2 She gets on the exercise bike after the running machine. (always)
3 The training session for teenagers is great fun. (usually)
4 I lift weights. (often)
5 The gym is busy in the evenings. (never)
6 We swim in the pool after the gym. (usually)

---

there is/are

UNIT 4 LESSON 1

Affirmative
There is a famous pier.
There are lots of attractions.
Negative
There isn't time.
There aren't any sharks in the sea.
Questions
Is there a place that everyone visits?
How many ghosts are there?
Are there any scary ones?

- We use *there is/are* to say that something exists.

PRACTICE: *there is/there are*

12 Complete with *there is/are*, or *there isn't/aren't*.

1 There _____ a river in Brighton. ✗
2 There _____ hundreds of great shops. ✓
3 There _____ any people in the sea. ✗
4 There _____ a restaurant on the pier. ✓
5 There _____ lots of tourists in the summer. ✓

13 Complete with *is/are there* and answer the questions.

1 ____ ____ a computer in your classroom?
2 ____ ____ lots of students at your school?
3 ____ ____ any girls in your class?
4 ____ ____ a swimming pool at your school?
5 How many students ____ ____ in your class?

Present continuous

UNIT 4 LESSONS 2 AND 3, UNIT 5 LESSON 1

Affirmative	
Full forms	**Contractions**
I am speaking.	I'm speaking.
You are speaking.	You're speaking.
He/She/It is speaking.	He's/She's/It's speaking.
We are speaking.	We're speaking.
They are speaking.	They're speaking.
Negative	**Contractions**
I am not speaking.	I'm not speaking.
He/She/It is not speaking.	He/She/It isn't speaking.
We/You/They are not speaking.	We/You/They aren't speaking.

Questions	Short answers
Am I speaking?	Yes, you are.
	No, you aren't.
Are you speaking?	Yes, I am.
	No, I'm not.
	Yes, we are.
	No, we aren't.
Is he/she/it speaking?	Yes, he/she/it is.
	No, he/she/it isn't.
Are they speaking?	Yes, they are.
	No, they aren't.

- We use the present continuous to talk about temporary events and what is happening **now**:
  It's raining.
  She's wearing a long grey coat.
  We're sailing from Spain to Barbados.
  She's having a wonderful time.
  Dolphins are playing around the boat at the moment.
  What's she doing?
  Are they dancing?
  They aren't dancing.
  Emily isn't singing.

- **Spelling**: verb + *ing*
  We add *ing* to most verbs:
  *stand – stand**ing**   hold – hold**ing***
  For verbs ending in *e*, we drop the *e* and add *ing*:
  *us**e** – us**ing**   com**e** – com**ing***
  Other verbs:
  *swim – swi**mm**ing   run – ru**nn**ing*
  *shop – sho**pp**ing   sit – si**tt**ing*

PRACTICE: Present continuous

14 Write sentences using the present continuous.

the actor/hold/a book
The actor is holding a book.

1 the guide/talk/to the group
2 the girls/watch/the woman
3 she/walk/out of the theatre
4 Katya/laugh/at Adam
5 I/do/this exercise
6 we/learn/English
7 you/wear/a nice top
8 the phone/ring

15 Complete with the present continuous.

1 Where ____ we ____? (go)
2 ____ you ____ hungry? (feel) Yes, I ____.
3 ____ the man ____? (cook) No, he ____.
4 ____ he ____ fish and chips? (sell) Yes, he ____.
5 What ____ the girl ____? (do).
6 She ____ ____. (not run)
7 ____ she ____ fast? (go) Yes, she ____.
8 The people ____ ____. (not dance)

16 Choose the present simple or present continuous.

1 I can hear music – Emily plays/is playing the saxophone.
2 How often do you go/are you going to the cinema?
3 We usually have/are having breakfast at 7.30.
4 I can't go swimming now – I do/I'm doing my homework.
5 It's a lovely day and the sun shines/is shining.
6 Adam starts/is starting school at nine in the morning.
7 The students work/are working on computers at the moment.
8 Do you like/Are you liking basketball?

Possessive adjectives and possessive pronouns
UNIT 5 LESSON 2

Possessive adjectives	Possessive pronouns
my	mine
your	yours
his/her	his/hers
our	ours
your	yours
their	theirs

- Possessive adjectives do not change with plural nouns:
  my book   **my** book**s**
- We do not use *the* before possessive pronouns:
  This book is ~~the~~ mine.
- We use the question word *Whose* to ask about possession:
  Whose turn is it?
  Whose books are these?

PRACTICE: Possessive adjectives and possessive pronouns

17 Complete with possessive pronouns.

These are Pierre's trainers. They're *his*.

1 That's my bag. It's _____.
2 This is our dinner. It's _____.
3 These are your CDs. They're _____.
4 The sunglasses are Adam's. They're _____.
5 They're Adam and Ruby's books. They're _____.
6 That guitar is Emily's. It's _____.

Possessive 's
UNIT 5 LESSON 2

- Singular nouns add *'s* (apostrophe *s*):
  *Adam**'s** turn   Teresa**'s** jeans*
- Irregular plural nouns also add *'s*:
  *people**'s** watches*
- Regular plural nouns add *'* after the *s*:
  *the student**s'** bags*

Comparative adjectives
UNIT 5 LESSON 3

Adjective	Comparative
1 syllable	
cold	cold**er**
high	high**er**
short	short**er**
late	lat**er**
1 syllable ending in single vowel + consonant	
big	bi**gger**
hot	ho**tter**
wet	we**tter**
1 or 2 syllables ending in *y*	
dry	dr**ier**
easy	eas**ier**
sunny	sunn**ier**

Adjective	Comparative
2 or more syllables	
difficult	**more** difficult
expensive	**more** expensive
famous	**more** famous
popular	**more** popular
Irregular	
good	**better**
bad	**worse**

- Short comparative adjectives end in *er*.
- Long comparative adjectives take *more* in front of them.

PRACTICE: **Comparative adjectives**

18 Write true sentences using comparative adjectives.

The tropics are sunnier than Antarctica.
Chinese is more difficult than English.

~~The tropics~~	big	~~Antarctica~~
~~Chinese~~	cold	~~English~~
London's population	~~difficult~~	Ruby's
Jake's hair	expensive	her rucksack
The Arctic	famous	Jennifer Lopez
A mobile phone	short	Brazil
Angelina Jolie	small	a calculator
Katya's bag	~~sunny~~	Zurich's

Past simple: *be*

UNIT 6 LESSON 1

Affirmative	Negative
I/he/she/it **was**	I/he/she/it **wasn't**
we/you/they **were**	we/you/they **weren't**
Questions	**Short answers**
Was I?/Were we?	Yes, you/we were.
	No, you/we weren't.
Were you?	Yes, I was.
	No, I wasn't.
Was he/she/it?	Yes, he/she/it was.
	No, he/she/it wasn't.
Were they?	Yes, they were.
	No, they weren't.

- There are only two past simple forms of *be*:
  She was in the park.
  They were on the beach.
  Jake wasn't at the cinema.
  We weren't at school.
  Contractions: *wasn't* = was not   *weren't* = were not
- In questions, the subject comes after *was/were*:
  Was Salvador Dalí from Spain?
  Where were you yesterday at noon?

PRACTICE: **Past simple** *be*

19 Complete the sentences with *was/wasn't* or *were/weren't*.

1 The girls _____ at the shopping centre. ✓
2 Teresa _____ in a bookshop. ✓
3 The students _____ at school. ✗
4 Mr Ward _____ in the classroom. ✗
5 He _____ at home. ✓

20 Complete the questions with *was/were* and answer them.

1 _____ Jake happy? Yes, he _____.
2 _____ Teresa with Emily? No, she _____.
3 _____ Adam and Ruby together? No, they _____.
4 Was I there? No, you _____.
5 _____ you late? No, we _____.

Past simple: regular and irregular verbs

UNIT 6 LESSONS 2 AND 3

Affirmative		Negative	
I		I	
you	played	you	didn't play
he/she/it	went	he/she/it	didn't go
we		we	
they			
Questions		**Short answers**	
Did you play …?		Yes, I/we did.	
		No, I/we didn't.	
Did he/she/it go …?		Yes, he/she/it did.	
		No, he/she/it didn't.	
Did they go …?		Yes, they did.	
		No, they didn't.	

- Regular and irregular verbs have only one affirmative form in the past simple.
- **Spelling:** affirmative forms of regular verbs
  We add *ed* to most verbs:
    cross**ed** discover**ed** play**ed** sail**ed** visit**ed**
  We add *d* to verbs ending in *e*:
    live**d** love**d**
  For verbs ending in a consonant and *y*, we drop the *y* and add *ied*:
    carry – carr**ied** study – stud**ied**
- Regular and irregular verbs form the negative and questions in the same way.
- Past simple negative: subject + *didn't* + verb:
  He didn't apologise.
  He didn't seem worried.
  I didn't say anything to him.
  Contraction: *didn't* = did not
- Past simple questions: *did* + subject + verb:
  Did Adam find the camera?
  Did you lose Pierre's camera?
  Did Pierre apologise?
  Did they visit Devil's Dyke?
- There is a complete list of all the irregular verbs in *New Inspiration 1* on page 127.

PRACTICE: Past simple regular and irregular verbs

21 Complete with the past simple of the verbs in the boxes.

> **Regular verbs**
> carry   like   live   play   sail   visit

1   Christopher Columbus _____ across the Atlantic in 1492.
2   We _____ Scandinavia last year.
3   I ___ the TV programme about Vikings last night.
4   Many Vikings _____ in Iceland and Greenland.
5   A Viking ship _____ lots of men.
6   Vikings _____ games in their free time.

> **Irregular verbs**
> come   find   go   have   make   wear

7   The Vikings _____ fair hair and blue eyes.
8   Viking women _____ long dresses.
9   Archaeologists _____ Viking jewellery in Britain.
10   Leif Eriksson _____ to America a thousand years ago.
11   Many Vikings _____ from Norway.
12   I _____ a Viking ship at primary school!

22 Look back at exercise 2 on page 80. Complete the questions and answer them.

1   _____ the group go to Devil's Dyke? _____, they _____.
2   _____ Teresa ask Pierre a question? _____, she _____.
3   _____ Teresa borrow Pierre's camera? _____, she _____.
4   _____ Teresa and Pierre talk about Adam? _____, they _____.
5   _____ Adam say sorry? _____, he _____.
6   _____ Adam find the camera? _____, he _____.

going to
UNIT 7 LESSON 1

Affirmative		Negative	
I'm		I'm not	
you're		you aren't	
he's		he isn't	
she's	going to	she isn't	going to
it's		it isn't	
we're		we aren't	
they're		they aren't	

Questions	Short answers
Are you going to?	Yes, I am. /Yes, we are. No, I'm not. /No, we aren't.
Is he/she/is going to?	Yes, he/she/it is. /No, he/she/ it isn't.
Are they going to?	Yes, they are. /No, they aren't.

• We use *going to* + infinitive to talk about future plans and intentions:
> *I am going to phone home.*
> *They are going to X-ray his leg.*
> *You are not going to be at the barbecue.*
> *Is he going to be all right?*
> *What are you going to do?*

PRACTICE: *going to*

23 Write sentences using *going to*.

he/phone home
He's going to phone home.

1   they/have a barbecue
2   what/you/wear?
3   I/wear my new jeans
4   what/he/do?
5   he/not/stay in Brighton
6   she/talk to him?
7   we/not/be late
8   they/not/forget him

Why...? because ...
UNIT 7 LESSON 1

• We use the linking word *because* to answer the question *Why ...?*
> *Why is Pierre wearing shorts?*
> *He's wearing shorts because he's going to play tennis.*

Verb + gerund
UNIT 7 LESSON 2

• A gerund is a noun formed from a verb. We can use a gerund after *like, love, enjoy, hate* and *don't mind*:
> *I love skateboard**ing**.*
> *She likes play**ing** video games.*
> *We enjoy swim**ming**.*
> *They like kni**tting**.*
> *He doesn't like danc**ing**.*
> *He doesn't mind jump**ing** out of a plane.*
> *What do they like do**ing**?*

PRACTICE: Verb + gerund

24 Complete with the correct form of the verb.

1   Pierre loves _____ volleyball. (play)
2   He also likes _____. (swim).
3   Do you like _____? (ride)
4   I don't mind _____. (cook)
5   We love _____. (skateboard)
6   Who hates _____ chess? (play)
7   My friends enjoy _____. (sail)
8   Lots of boys don't like _____. (dance)

Superlative adjectives
UNIT 7 LESSON 3

Adjective	Superlative
1 syllable	
fast	the fast**est**
slow	the slow**est**
strange	the strang**est**
1 syllable ending in single vowel + consonant	
big	the big**gest**
hot	the hot**test**
1 or 2 syllables ending in *y*	
dry	the dri**est**
friendly	the friendl**iest**

Adjective	Superlative
2 or more syllables	
dangerous	the **most** dangerous
beautiful	the **most** beautiful
Irregular	
good	the **best**
bad	the **worst**

- Short superlative adjectives end in *est*.
- Long superlative adjectives take *most* in front of them.

PRACTICE: Superlative adjectives

25 Complete with the superlative form of the adjectives.

1 The _____ bird is the falcon. (fast)
2 The _____ snake is the Indian cobra. (dangerous)
3 Is the hippo the _____ animal in the world? (big)
4 Which band do you like most? Which is the _____? (good)
5 I hated it. It was the _____ film this year. (bad)
6 Which is the _____ animal in the world? (exciting)

---

some and *any*

UNIT 8 LESSON 1

- We use *some* and *any* with both plural and uncountable nouns.
- We use *some* in affirmative sentences:
    There's some apple juice in the fridge.
    You ate some meat last night.
    Let's make some kebabs.
  and in questions when we are making offers:
    Would you like some tea?
- We use *any* in negative sentences and neutral questions:
    Are there any bananas?
    I don't want any meat.

PRACTICE: *some* and *any*

26 Complete with *some* or *any*.

1 I'd like _____ bread and cheese.
2 I don't want _____ sausages.
3 Are there _____ apples?
4 Let's make _____ hamburgers.
5 I'd like _____ carrots, please.
6 There isn't _____ milk on the table.
7 Is there _____ meat in the fridge?
8 Would you like _____ sandwiches?

Countable and uncountable nouns

UNIT 8 LESSON 1

- Countable nouns have a singular and a plural form:
    an apple – apples   a sandwich – sandwiches
- We don't use *a/an* with uncountable nouns:
    We like cheese.   Do you want some bread?
- Uncountable nouns are singular:
    *Bread **is**n't expensive.   Milk **comes** from cows.*

---

have got

UNIT 8 LESSON 2

Affirmative	Contractions
I/you/we/they **have got**	I/you/we/they**'ve got**
he/she/it **has got**	he/she/it**'s got**
Negative	
I/you/we/they **have not got**	I/you/we/they **haven't got**
he/she/it **has not got**	he/she/it **hasn't got**
Questions	**Short answers**
Has he **got** a games console?	Yes, he **has**. No, he **hasn't**.
Have they **got** phones?	Yes, they **have**. No, they **haven't**.
Who **has got** a job?	I **have**.

- We use *have got* like *have* to talk about possession. There is no continuous form.

PRACTICE: *have got*

27 Complete with the correct form of *have got*.

1 Katya _____ a brother and sister.
2 _____ Jake _____ short hair?
3 Ruby _____ (not) a boyfriend.
4 Adam and Jake _____ camera phones.
5 I _____ (not) their numbers.
6 We _____ (not) a lot of money.
7 Don't run! You _____ lots of time.
8 _____ Emily _____ a sax?
9 _____ Ruby and Pierre _____ the same colour eyes?
10 Who _____ my DVD?

Question tags with *be*

UNIT 8 LESSON 3

- We can use question tags with **falling** intonation to ask for agreement when we are sure about something:
    ***It's** a great party, **isn't it**?*
    ***You're** Teresa, **aren't you**?*
    ***She's** sad, **isn't she**?*
    ***They're** having fun, **aren't they**?*
  BUT   ***I'm** late, **aren't I**?*
- When the statement in the first part of the sentence is affirmative, the question tag is negative.
- We can use question tags with **rising** intonation to ask real questions:
    It's his birthday soon, isn't it?

PRACTICE: question tags with *be*

28 Complete with question tags.

1 Pierre is from Geneva, _____?
2 Emily and Adam are English, _____?
3 We're teenagers, _____?
4 Katya is blonde, _____?
5 Teresa's surname is Navarro, _____?
6 You're a student, _____?
7 I'm right, _____?

WORD LIST

★ = fairly common words   ★★ = very common words   ★★★ = the most common and basic words

WELCOME! & UNIT 1

address (n) ★★★	/ə'dres/
bike ride (n)	/'baɪk ˌraɪd/
birthday (n) ★★	/'bɜːθdeɪ/
cat (n) ★★★	/kæt/
copy (n) ★★★	/'kɒpi/
day (n) ★★★	/deɪ/
disco (n) ★	/'dɪskəʊ/
everyone (pron) ★★★	/'evriˌwʌn/
exchange (n) ★★★	/ɪks'tʃeɪndʒ/
film (n) ★★★	/fɪlm/
friend (n) ★★★	/frend/
here (adv) ★★★	/hɪə/
information (n) ★★★	/ˌɪnfə'meɪʃ(ə)n/
language (n) ★★★	/'læŋgwɪdʒ/
lunch (n) ★★★	/lʌntʃ/
music (n) ★★★	/'mjuːzɪk/
name (n) ★★★	/neɪm/
now (adv) ★★★	/naʊ/
party (n) ★★★	/'pɑːti/
phone number (n) ★	/'fəʊn ˌnʌmbə/
photographer (n) ★★	/fə'tɒgrəfə/
Please. ★★★	/pliːz/
population (n) ★★★	/ˌpɒpjʊ'leɪʃ(ə)n/
present (n) ★★★	/'prez(ə)nt/
programme (n) ★★★	/'prəʊgræm/
singer (n) ★★	/'sɪŋə/
song (n) ★★★	/sɒŋ/
student (n) ★★★	/'stjuːd(ə)nt/
surname (n) ★	/'sɜːneɪm/
teacher (n) ★★★	/'tiːtʃə/
thing (n) ★★★	/θɪŋ/
tour (n) ★★★	/tʊə/
turn (n) ★★★	/tɜːn/
very (adv) ★★★	/'veri/
visit (n) ★★★	/'vɪzɪt/
visitor (n) ★★★	/'vɪzɪtə/
welcome (n) ★★	/'welkəm/

ADJECTIVES

beautiful (adj) ★★★	/'bjuːtəf(ə)l/
famous (adj) ★★★	/'feɪməs/
favourite (adj) ★★	/'feɪv(ə)rət/
fine (adj) ★★★	/faɪn/
great (adj) ★★★	/greɪt/
international (adj) ★★★	/ˌɪntə'næʃ(ə)nəl/
main (adj) ★★★	/meɪn/
new (adj) ★★★	/njuː/
nice (adj) ★★★	/naɪs/
OK (adj) ★★★	/ˌəʊ'keɪ/
old (adj) ★★★	/əʊld/
pleased (adj) ★★	/pliːzd/
right (adj) ★★★	/raɪt/
sorry (adj) ★★★	/'sɒri/

COUNTRIES

Australia	/ɒ'streɪliə/
Brazil	/brə'zɪl/
China	/'tʃaɪnə/
Egypt	/'iːdʒɪpt/
England	/'ɪŋglənd/
Germany	/'dʒɜːməni/
India	/'ɪndiə/
Mexico	/'meksɪkəʊ/
Peru	/pə'ruː/
Russia	/'rʌʃə/
Spain	/speɪn/
Switzerland	/'swɪtsələnd/
the USA	/ðə juːes'eɪ/
(United States of America)	
Turkey	/'tɜːki/

FAMILY

boy (n) ★★★	/bɔɪ/
boyfriend (n) ★★	/'bɔɪˌfrend/
brother (n) ★★★	/'brʌðə/
child (pl children) (n) ★★★	/tʃaɪld/
daughter (n) ★★★	/'dɔːtə/
family (n) ★★★	/'fæm(ə)li/
father (n) ★★★	/'fɑːðə/
girl (n) ★★★	/gɜːl/
girlfriend (n) ★★	/'gɜːl,frend/
grandfather (n) ★★	/'græn(d),fɑːðə/
grandmother (n) ★★	/'græn(d),mʌðə/
grandparent (n) ★	/'græn(d),peərənt/
husband (n) ★★★	/'hʌzbənd/
man (pl men) (n) ★★★	/mæn/
mother (n) ★★★	/'mʌðə/
Mr ★★★	/'mɪstə/
Mrs ★★★	/'mɪsɪz/
mum (n) ★★	/mʌm/
parent (n) ★★★	/'peərənt/
person (pl people) (n) ★★★	/'pɜːs(ə)n/
sister (n) ★★★	/'sɪstə/
son (n) ★★★	/sʌn/
wife (pl wives) (n) ★★★	/waɪf/

MONTHS OF THE YEAR

January ★★★	/'dʒænjuəri/
February ★★★	/'februəri/
March ★★★	/mɑːtʃ/
April ★★★	/'eɪprəl/
May ★★★	/meɪ/
June ★★★	/dʒuːn/
July ★★★	/dʒʊ'laɪ/
August ★★★	/'ɔːgəst/
September ★★★	/sep'tembə/
October ★★★	/ɒk'təʊbə/
November ★★★	/nəʊ'vembə/
December ★★★	/dɪ'sembə/

NUMBERS TO 1,000,000

oh	/əʊ/
zero ★★	/'zɪərəʊ/
one ★★★	/wʌn/
two ★★★	/tuː/
three ★★★	/θriː/
four ★★★	/fɔː/
five ★★★	/faɪv/
six	/sɪks/
seven	/'sev(ə)n/
eight	/eɪt/
nine	/naɪn/
ten	/ten/
eleven	/ɪ'lev(ə)n/
twelve	/twelv/
thirteen	/θɜː'tiːn/
fourteen	/fɔː'tiːn/
fifteen	/fɪf'tiːn/
sixteen	/sɪks'tiːn/
seventeen	/ˌsev(ə)n'tiːn/
eighteen	/eɪ'tiːn/
nineteen	/ˌnaɪn'tiːn/
twenty	/'twenti/
thirty	/'θɜːti/
forty	/'fɔːti/
fifty	/'fɪfti/
sixty	/'sɪksti/
seventy	/'sev(ə)nti/
eighty	/'eɪti/
ninety	/'naɪnti/
a hundred ★★	/ə 'hʌndrəd/
a thousand ★★	/ə 'θaʊzənd/
a million ★★	/ə 'mɪljən/

ORDINAL NUMBERS

first ★★★	/fɜːst/
second ★★★	/'sekənd/
third ★★★	/θɜːd/
fourth ★★★	/fɔːθ/
fifth ★★★	/fɪfθ/
sixth ★★★	/sɪksθ/
seventh ★★★	/'sev(ə)nθ/
eighth ★★★	/eɪtθ/
ninth ★★★	/naɪnθ/
tenth ★★★	/tenθ/
eleventh	/ɪ'lev(ə)nθ/
twelfth	/twelfθ/
thirteenth	/θɜː'tiːnθ/
fourteenth	/ˌfɔː'tiːnθ/
fifteenth	/ˌfɪf'tiːnθ/
sixteenth	/ˌsɪks'tiːnθ/
seventeenth	/ˌsev(ə)n'tiːnθ/
eighteenth	/eɪ'tiːnθ/
nineteenth	/ˌnaɪn'tiːnθ/
twentieth	/'twentiəθ/
twenty-first	/ˌtwenti'fɜːst/
twenty-second	/ˌtwenti'sekənd/
thirtieth	/'θɜːtiəθ/
fortieth	/'fɔːtiəθ/

PLACES AND BUILDINGS

beach (n) ★★★	/biːtʃ/
building (n) ★★★	/'bɪldɪŋ/
capital (city) (n) ★★★	/'kæpɪt(ə)l/
centre (n) ★★★	/'sentə/
city (n) ★★★	/'sɪti/
country (n) ★★★	/'kʌntri/
mountain (n) ★★★	/'maʊntɪn/
place (n) ★★★	/pleɪs/
river (n) ★★★	/'rɪvə/
road (n) ★★★	/rəʊd/
school (n) ★★★	/skuːl/
street (n) ★★★	/striːt/
temple (n) ★★	/'temp(ə)l/

POSSESSIONS

alarm clock (n) ★★	/ə'lɑːm ˌklɒk/
bag (n) ★★★	/bæg/
bicycle (n) ★★	/'baɪsɪk(ə)l/
bottle of water (n)	/ˌbɒtl əv 'wɔːtə/
calculator (n) ★	/'kælkjʊˌleɪtə/
CD (n) ★★	/ˌsiː'diː/
clock (n) ★★	/klɒk/
comb (n) ★	/kəʊm/
digital camera (n)	/ˌdɪdʒɪtl 'kæmrə/
ID card (n)	/aɪ'diː kɑːd/
key (n) ★★★	/kiː/
map (n) ★★★	/mæp/
mobile phone (n) ★★	/ˌməʊbaɪl 'fəʊn/
MP3 player (n)	/ˌempiː'θriː ˌpleɪə/
packet of tissues (n)	/ˌpækɪt əv 'tɪʃuːz/
passport (n) ★	/'pɑːspɔːt/
pen (n) ★★	/pen/
photo (n) ★★	/'fəʊtəʊ/
photograph (n) ★★★	/'fəʊtəˌgrɑːf/
picture (n) ★★★	/'pɪktʃə/
rucksack (n)	/'rʌkˌsæk/
ticket (n) ★★★	/'tɪkɪt/
umbrella (n) ★	/ʌm'brelə/
wallet (n)	/'wɒlɪt/
watch (n) ★★	/wɒtʃ/

PREPOSITIONS OF PLACE

at (prep) ★★★	/æt, ət/
in (prep) ★★★	/ɪn/
near (prep) ★★★	/nɪə/
next to (prep)	/'nekst ˌtuː/
on (prep) ★★★	/ɒn/
on the left/right	/ˌɒn ðə 'left/'raɪt/
over there	/ˌəʊvə 'ðeə/

TIME

at (prep) ★★★	/æt, ət/
at the same time	/ət ðə seɪm 'taɪm/
for (prep) ★★★	/fɔː, fə/
half past (adv)	/'hɑːf ˌpɑːst/
month (n) ★★★	/mʌnθ/
o'clock (adv) ★★	/ə'klɒk/
on (prep) ★★★	/ɒn/
quarter past/to (adv)	/'kwɔːtə ˌpɑːst/ˌtuː/
today (adv) ★★★	/tə'deɪ/
tonight (adv) ★★★	/tə'naɪt/
year (n) ★★★	/jɪə/

VERBS

be (v) ★★★	/biː, bi/
believe (v) ★★★	/bɪ'liːv/

check (v) ★★★ /tʃek/
guess (v) ★★★ /ges/
know (v) ★★★ /nəʊ/
listen (v) ★★★ /'lɪs(ə)n/
look (v) ★★★ /lʊk/
mean (v) ★★★ /miːn/
meet (v) ★★★ /miːt/
pronounce (v) ★★ /prə'naʊns/
spell (v) ★★ /spel/
think (v) ★★★ /θɪŋk/

EXPRESSIONS

Excuse me. /ɪk'skjuːz ˌmiː/
How do you spell it? /ˌhaʊ du jʊ 'spel ɪt/
I see. /ˌaɪ 'siː/
It's called … /ˌɪts 'kɔːld/
of course ★★★ /əv 'kɔːs/
Thank you (very much) /'θæŋk juː (veri mʌtʃ)/
   ★★★
That's right. /ˌðæts 'raɪt/
What else? /ˌwɒt 'els/

UNIT 2

also (adv) ★★★ /'ɔːlsəʊ/
anything (pron) ★★★ /'eniˌθɪŋ/
bed (n) ★★★ /bed/
behind (prep) ★★★ /bɪ'haɪnd/
book (n) ★★★ /bʊk/
button (n) ★★ /'bʌt(ə)n/
cake (n) ★★★ /keɪk/
century (n) ★★★ /'sentʃəri/
date (n) ★★★ /deɪt/
dictionary (n) ★★ /'dɪkʃən(ə)ri/
door (n) ★★★ /dɔː/
drink (n) ★★★ /drɪŋk/
first (adv) ★★★ /fɜːst/
flag (n) ★★ /flæg/
football (n) ★★★ /'fʊtˌbɔːl/
at home (adv) /ət həʊm/
horse (n) ★★★ /hɔːs/
house (n) ★★★ /haʊs/
kilo(gram) (kg) (n) ★ /'kiːləʊ (græm)/
kilometre (km) (n) ★ /'kɪləˌmiːtə, kɪ'lɒmɪtə/
late (adj & adv) ★★★ /leɪt/
later (See you later.) /'leɪtə/
   (adv) ★★★
life (pl lives) (n) ★★★ /laɪf/
light (n) ★★★ /laɪt/
light switch (n) /'laɪt ˌswɪtʃ/
lots (of) (n pl) ★★★ /lɒts (əv)/
meal (n) ★★★ /miːl/
member (n) ★★★ /'membə/
message (n) ★★★ /'mesɪdʒ/
metre (n) ★★★ /'miːtə/
minute (n) ★★★ /'mɪnɪt/
over here /ˌəʊvə 'hɪə/
problem (n) ★★★ /'prɒbləm/
puncture (n) /'pʌŋktʃə/
question (n) ★★★ /'kwestʃ(ə)n/
questionnaire (n) ★★ /ˌkwestʃə'neə/
really (= very) (adv) /'rɪəli/
   ★★★
reply (n) ★★★ /rɪ'plaɪ/
room (n) ★★★ /ruːm/
round (prep) ★★★ /raʊnd/
shoulder bag (n) /'ʃəʊldə ˌbæg/
skill (n) ★★★ /skɪl/
smile (n) ★★★ /smaɪl/
someone (pron) ★★★ /'sʌmwʌn/
something (pron) ★★★ /'sʌmθɪŋ/
sound (n) ★★★ /saʊnd/
sunglasses (n pl) /'sʌnˌglɑːsɪz/
then (adv) ★★★ /ðen/
toilet (n) ★★ /'tɔɪlət/
tomorrow (adv) ★★★ /tə'mɒrəʊ/
underwater (adv) /ˌʌndə'wɔːtə/
wall (n) ★★★ /wɔːl/
whole (n) ★★★ /həʊl/
window (n) ★★★ /'wɪndəʊ/
word (n) ★★★ /wɜːd/

ADJECTIVES

big (adj) ★★★ /bɪg/
blonde (adj) ★ /blɒnd/
cool (adj) ★★★ /kuːl/
dark (adj) ★★★ /dɑːk/

easy (adj) ★★★ /'iːzi/
expensive (adj) /ɪk'spensɪv/
fantastic (adj) ★★ /fæn'tæstɪk/
good (adj) ★★★ /gʊd/
long (adj) ★★★ /lɒŋ/
lovely (adj) ★★★ /'lʌvli/
lucky (adj) ★★★ /'lʌki/
national (adj) ★★★ /'næʃ(ə)nəl/
open (adj) ★★★ /'əʊpən/
other (adj) ★★★ /'ʌðə/
same (adj) ★★★ /seɪm/
short (adj) ★★★ /ʃɔːt/
silly (adj) ★★ /'sɪli/
special (adj) /'speʃl/
sure (adj) ★★★ /ʃɔː, ʃʊə/
wrong (adj) ★★★ /rɒŋ/

CLOTHES

cap (n) ★★ /kæp/
clothes (n pl) ★★★ /kləʊðz/
jacket (n) ★★★ /'dʒækɪt/
jeans (n pl) ★ /dʒiːnz/
pair (of jeans) (n) ★★★ /peə/
pullover (n) ★ /'pʊləʊvə/
sandals (n pl) /'sændəlz/
scarf (n) ★ /skɑːf/
shirt (n) ★★★ /ʃɜːt/
shoes (n pl) ★★★ /ʃuːz/
shorts (n pl) ★ /ʃɔːts/
skirt (n) ★★ /skɜːt/
socks (n pl) ★ /sɒks/
T-shirt (n) ★ /'tiːʃɜːt/
top (n) ★★★ /tɒp/
trainers (n pl) ★ /'treɪnəz/
trousers (n pl) ★★ /'traʊzəz/

COLOURS

black (adj) ★★★ /blæk/
blue (adj) ★★★ /bluː/
brown (adj) ★★★ /braʊn/
colour (n) ★★★ /'kʌlə/
green (adj) ★★★ /griːn/
grey (adj) ★★★ /greɪ/
orange (adj) ★★ /'ɒrɪndʒ/
pink (adj) ★★★ /pɪŋk/
purple (adj) ★ /'pɜːp(ə)l/
red (adj) ★★★ /red/
white (adj) ★★★ /waɪt/
yellow (adj) ★★★ /'jeləʊ/

COMMUNICATION AND TECHNOLOGY

area code (n) /'eəriə ˌkəʊd/
audio (n) /'ɔːdiəʊ/
burn a CD /ˌbɜːn ə siː'diː/
code (n) ★★★ /kəʊd/
computer (n) ★★★ /kəm'pjuːtə/
dial (v) ★ /'daɪəl/
download (v) /ˌdaʊn'ləʊd/
laptop (n) /'læpˌtɒp/
menu (n) ★★ /'menjuː/
microphone (n) ★ /'maɪkrəˌfəʊn/
mobile (phone) (n) ★★ /'məʊbaɪl/
number (n) ★★★ /'nʌmbə/
phone (n & v) ★★★ /fəʊn/
phone call (n) ★ /'fəʊn ˌkɔːl/
programme (v) /'prəʊgræm/
satnav (n) /'sætˌnæv/
site (n) ★★ /saɪt/
social networking /ˌsəʊʃ(ə)l 'netˌwɜːkɪŋ saɪt/
   site (n)
speakers (n pl) /'spiːkəz/
text message (n) /'tekst ˌmesɪdʒ/
video (n) ★★★ /'vɪdiəʊ/
video call (n) /'vɪdiəʊ ˌkɔːl/
Web (n) ★ /web/
web page (n) ★ /'web ˌpeɪdʒ/
webcam (n) /'webˌkæm/
website (n) ★★ /'webˌsaɪt/

MUSIC

band (n) ★★★ /bænd/
drums (n pl) ★★ /drʌmz/
gig (n) ★ /gɪg/
guitar (n) ★★★ /gɪ'tɑː/
instrument (n) ★★★ /'ɪnstrʊmənt/

piano (n) ★★ /pi'ænəʊ/
saxophone (n) /'sæksəˌfəʊn/

PARTS OF THE BODY

back (n) ★★★ /bæk/
eye (n) ★★★ /aɪ/
face (n) ★★★ /feɪs/
hair (n) ★★★ /heə/
hand (n) ★★★ /hænd/
neck (n) ★★★ /nek/

VERBS

ask (v) ★★★ /ɑːsk/
borrow (v) ★★ /'bɒrəʊ/
choose (v) ★★★ /tʃuːz/
close (v) ★★★ /kləʊz/
come (v) ★★★ /kʌm/
cook (v) ★★★ /kʊk/
create (v) ★★★ /kri'eɪt/
dance (v) ★★★ /dɑːns/
draw (v) ★★★ /drɔː/
find (v) ★★★ /faɪnd/
forget (v) ★★★ /fə'get/
get (v) ★★★ /get/
give (v) ★★★ /gɪv/
go (v) ★★★ /gəʊ/
have (v) ★★★ /hæv, əv, həv/
help (n & v) ★★★ /help/
iron (v) ★ /'aɪən/
leave (v) ★★★ /liːv/
lift (v) ★★★ /lɪft/
like (v) ★★★ /laɪk/
love (v) ★★★ /lʌv/
make (v) ★★★ /meɪk/
mend (v) ★ /mend/
move around (v) /ˌmuːv ə'raʊnd/
open (v) ★★★ /'əʊpən/
paint (v) ★★★ /peɪnt/
play (music) (v) ★★★ /pleɪ/
read (v) ★★★ /riːd/
remember (v) ★★★ /rɪ'membə/
ride (v) ★★★ /raɪd/
run (v) ★★★ /rʌn/
say (v) ★★★ /seɪ/
see (v) ★★★ /siː/
select (v) ★★★ /sɪ'lekt/
send (v) ★★★ /send/
sew on (v) /ˌsəʊ 'ɒn/
sing (v) ★★★ /sɪŋ/
sit (v) ★★★ /sɪt/
speak (v) ★★★ /spiːk/
swim (v) ★★ /swɪm/
talk (v) ★★★ /tɔːk/
understand (v) ★★★ /ˌʌndə'stænd/
use (v) ★★★ /juːz/
walk (v) ★★★ /wɔːk/

EXPRESSIONS

Don't worry. /ˌdəʊnt 'wʌri/
go home /ˌgəʊ 'həʊm/
Keep still. /ˌkiːp 'stɪl/
make sure /ˌmeɪk 'ʃɔː/
Never mind. /ˌnevə 'maɪnd/
No problem. /ˌnəʊ 'prɒbləm/
Oh dear. /ˌəʊ 'dɪə/
take a picture /ˌteɪk ə 'pɪktʃə/
tell a joke /ˌtel ə 'dʒəʊk/
Thanks (a lot). /θæŋks (ə lɒt)/
There's something /ˌðeəz sʌmθɪŋ 'rɒŋ/
   wrong.

UNIT 3

again (adv) ★★★ /ə'gen/
backyard (n) /ˌbæk'jɑːd/
between (prep) ★★★ /bɪ'twiːn/
boat (n) ★★★ /bəʊt/
both (pron) ★★★ /bəʊθ/
break (n) ★★★ /breɪk/
car (n) ★★★ /kɑː/
chicken (n) ★★ /'tʃɪkɪn/
cottage (n) ★★ /'kɒtɪdʒ/
dad (n) ★★ /dæd/
email (n) ★★★ /'iːmeɪl/
epal (n) /'iːpæl/
everything (pron) ★★★ /'evriˌθɪŋ/

WORD LIST

except (prep) ★★★ /ɪkˈsept/
field (n) ★★★ /fiːld/
film star (n) /ˈfɪlm ˌstɑː/
flat (n) ★★★ /flæt/
garden (n) ★★★ /ˈgɑːd(ə)n/
inside (adv) ★★★ /ˈɪnˌsaɪd/
like (prep) ★★★ /laɪk/
money (n) ★★★ /ˈmʌni/
newspaper (n) ★★★ /ˈnjuːzˌpeɪpə/
only (adv) ★★★ /ˈəʊnli/
outdoors (adv) /ˌaʊtˈdɔːz/
outside (prep) ★★★ /ˌaʊtˈsaɪd/
over (prep) ★★★ /ˈəʊvə/
routine (n) ★★ /ruːˈtiːn/
quite (adv) ★★★ /kwaɪt/
sea (n) ★★★ /siː/
summer (n) ★★★ /ˈsʌmə/
sweatshirt (n) /ˈswetˌʃɜːt/
teenager (n) ★★ /ˈtiːnˌeɪdʒə/
town (n) ★★★ /taʊn/
training session (n) /ˈtreɪnɪŋ ˌseʃn/
uniform (n) ★★ /ˈjuːnɪfɔːm/
winter (n) ★★★ /ˈwɪntə/
world (n) ★★★ /wɜːld/

ADJECTIVES

aged (adj) ★★ /ˈeɪdʒd/
angry (adj) ★★★ /ˈæŋgri/
born (adj) ★★★ /bɔːn/
busy (adj) ★★★ /ˈbɪzi/
different (adj) ★★★ /ˈdɪfrənt/
free (= costs nothing) /friː/
   (adj) ★★★
fresh (adj) ★★★ /freʃ/
local (adj) ★★★ /ˈləʊk(ə)l/
mental (adj) ★★★ /ˈment(ə)l/
own (adj) ★★★ /əʊn/
physical (adj) ★★★ /ˈfɪzɪk(ə)l/
poor (adj) ★★★ /pɔː, pʊə/
popular (adj) ★★★ /ˈpɒpjʊlə/
ready (adj) ★★★ /ˈredi/
regular (adj) ★★★ /ˈregjʊlə/
small (adj) ★★★ /smɔːl/
spicy (adj) /ˈspaɪsi/
teenage (adj) ★★ /ˈtiːnˌeɪdʒ/

COMPASS POINTS

east (n) ★★★ /iːst/
north (n) ★★★ /nɔːθ/
south (n) ★★★ /saʊθ/
west (n) ★★★ /west/

FOOD AND DRINK

banana (n) ★ /bəˈnɑːnə/
breakfast (n) ★★★ /ˈbrekfəst/
carrot (n) ★ /ˈkærət/
cheese (n) ★★ /tʃiːz/
chips (n pl) /tʃɪps/
chocolate (n) ★★ /ˈtʃɒklət/
cucumber (n) /ˈkjuːˌkʌmbə/
dinner (n) ★★★ /ˈdɪnə/
egg (n) ★★★ /eg/
fish (n) ★★★ /fɪʃ/
food (n) ★★★ /fuːd/
fruit (n) ★★★ /fruːt/
garlic (n) ★ /ˈgɑːlɪk/
ice cream (n) ★ /ˈaɪs ˌkriːm/
meat (n) ★★★ /miːt/
meatball (n) /ˈmiːtˌbɔːl/
menu (n) ★★ /ˈmenjuː/
mushroom (n) ★ /ˈmʌʃruːm/
octopus (n) /ˈɒktəpəs/
pizza (n) ★ /ˈpiːtsə/
potato (n) ★★ /pəˈteɪtəʊ/
salad (n) ★★ /ˈsæləd/
snack (n) ★ /snæk/
soup (n) ★★ /suːp/
tomato (n) ★★ /təˈmɑːtəʊ/

DAYS OF THE WEEK

Monday ★★★ /ˈmʌndeɪ/
Tuesday ★★★ /ˈtjuːzdeɪ/
Wednesday ★★★ /ˈwenzdeɪ/
Thursday ★★★ /ˈθɜːzdeɪ/
Friday ★★★ /ˈfraɪdeɪ/

Saturday ★★★ /ˈsætədeɪ/
Sunday ★★★ /ˈsʌndeɪ/

MUSIC

blues (n) ★ /bluːz/
hip-hop (n) /ˈhɪpˌhɒp/
jazz (n) ★ /dʒæz/
R&B (n) /ˌɑːrənˈbiː/
rapper (n) /ˈræpə/
reggae (n) /ˈregeɪ/
rock (music) (n) ★★★ /rɒk/

SCHOOL

class (n) ★★★ /klɑːs/
classroom (n) ★★ /ˈklɑːsˌruːm/
headmaster (n) ★ /ˌhedˈmɑːstə/
homework (n) ★ /ˈhəʊmˌwɜːk/
lesson (n) ★★★ /ˈles(ə)n/
timetable (n) ★★ /ˈtaɪmˌteɪb(ə)l/

SCHOOL SUBJECTS

art (n) ★★★ /ɑːt/
biology (n) ★ /baɪˈɒlədʒi/
computer studies (n) /kəmˈpjuːtə ˌstʌdiz/
geography (n) ★★ /dʒiːˈɒgrəfi/
history (n) ★★★ /ˈhɪst(ə)ri/
maths (n) ★ /mæθs/
music (n) ★★★ /ˈmjuːzɪk/
PE (physical /ˌpiː ˈiː/
   education) (n)
science (n) ★★★ /ˈsaɪəns/

SPORT, THE GYM AND LEISURE ACTIVITIES

activity (n) ★★★ /ækˈtɪvəti/
basketball (n) ★ /ˈbɑːskɪtˌbɔːl/
cinema (n) ★★ /ˈsɪnəmə/
computer game (n) /kəmˈpjuːtə ˌgeɪm/
dance (n) ★★★ /dɑːns/
dance routine (n) /ˈdɑːns ruːˌtiːn/
exercise (n) ★★★ /ˈeksəsaɪz/
exercise bike (n) /ˈeksəsaɪz ˌbaɪk/
fitness (n) ★★ /ˈfɪtnəs/
free time /friː ˌtaɪm/
game (n) ★★★ /geɪm/
go dancing /ˌgəʊ ˈdɑːnsɪŋ/
go rollerblading /ˌgəʊ ˈrəʊləbleɪdɪŋ/
go running /ˌgəʊ ˈrʌnɪŋ/
go shopping /ˌgəʊ ˈʃɒpɪŋ/
go skiing /ˌgəʊ ˈskiːɪŋ/
go swimming /ˌgəʊ ˈswɪmɪŋ/
goal (n) ★★★ /gəʊl/
golf (n) ★★★ /gɒlf/
gym (n) ★ /dʒɪm/
gymnastics (n) /dʒɪmˈnæstɪks/
holiday(s) (n) ★★★ /ˈhɒlɪdeɪ(z)/
jive (n) /dʒaɪv/
motor racing (n) /ˈməʊtə ˌreɪsɪŋ/
movie (n) ★ /ˈmuːvi/
net (n) ★★★ /net/
pool (= game) (n) /puːl/
rowing machine (n) /ˈrəʊɪŋ məˌʃiːn/
running machine (n) /ˈrʌnɪŋ məˌʃiːn/
skate (n) ★ /skeɪt/
sport (n) ★★★ /spɔːt/
swimming (n) ★ /ˈswɪmɪŋ/
swimming pool (n) /ˈswɪmɪŋ ˌpuːl/
   ★★★
team (n) ★★★ /tiːm/
ten-pin bowling (n) /ˌtenpɪn ˈbəʊlɪŋ/
tennis (n) ★★ /ˈtenɪs/
tennis court (n) /ˈtenɪs ˌkɔːt/
tennis racket (n) /ˈtenɪs ˌrækɪt/
TV (television) (n) ★★★ /ˌtiː ˈviː/
volleyball (n) /ˈvɒliˌbɔːl/
weights (n) /weɪts/
yoga (n) /ˈjəʊgə/

TIME

after (prep) ★★★ /ˈɑːftə/
afternoon (n) ★★★ /ˌɑːftəˈnuːn/
am (= in the morning) /eɪˈem/
before (prep) ★★★ /bɪˈfɔː/
early (adv) ★★★ /ˈɜːli/
evening (n) ★★★ /ˈiːvnɪŋ/

from (time) to (time) /frəm (taɪm) tə (taɪm)/
   (prep)
hour (n) ★★★ /ˈaʊə/
long (40 minutes /lɒŋ/
   long) (adv) ★★★
morning (n) ★★★ /ˈmɔːnɪŋ/
night (n) ★★★ /naɪt/
pm (= in the /piːˈem/
   afternoon/evening)
soon (adv) ★★★ /suːn/
week (n) ★★★ /wiːk/
weekday (n) /ˈwiːkdeɪ/
weekend (n) ★★★ /ˌwiːkˈend/

VERBS

buy (v) ★★★ /baɪ/
clean (v) ★★★ /kliːn/
do (v) ★★★ /duː/
drive (v) ★★★ /draɪv/
eat (v) ★★★ /iːt/
end (v) ★★★ /end/
enjoy (v) ★★★ /ɪnˈdʒɔɪ/
hate (v) ★★★ /heɪt/
hear (v) ★★★ /hɪə/
hope (v) ★★★ /həʊp/
learn (v) ★★★ /lɜːn/
live (v) ★★★ /lɪv/
pay (v) ★★★ /peɪ/
play (sport) (v) ★★★ /pleɪ/
race (v) ★★ /reɪs/
sleep (v) ★★★ /sliːp/
sound (v) ★★★ /saʊnd/
start (v) ★★★ /stɑːt/
stay (v) ★★★ /steɪ/
stop (v) ★★★ /stɒp/
study (v) ★★★ /ˈstʌdi/
teach (v) ★★★ /tiːtʃ/
visit (v) ★★★ /ˈvɪzɪt/
want (v) ★★★ /wɒnt/
watch (v) ★★★ /wɒtʃ/
work (v) ★★★ /wɜːk/
write (v) ★★★ /raɪt/

EXPRESSIONS

best wishes /ˌbest ˈwɪʃəz/
It depends. /ɪt dɪˈpendz/
get on (a bike) /ˌget ˈɒn (ə baɪk)/
get up /ˌget ˈʌp/
go away /ˌgəʊ əˈweɪ/
go to bed /ˌgəʊ tə ˈbed/
go to the cinema/ /ˌgəʊ tə ðə ˈsɪnəmə/
   movies /ˈmuːviz/
have breakfast/lunch/ /ˌhæv ˈbrekfəst/ˈlʌntʃ/
   dinner /ˈdɪnə/
What does he look /ˌwɒt dəz hiː ˈlʊk laɪk/
   like?
Why not? /ˌwaɪ ˈnɒt/
work hard /ˌwɜːk ˈhɑːd/

UNIT 4

actor (n) ★★★ /ˈæktə/
air (n) ★★★ /eə/
bedroom (n) ★★★ /ˈbedruːm/
coast (n) ★★★ /kəʊst/
coat (n) ★★★ /kəʊt/
coffin (n) ★★ /ˈkɒfɪn/
down (adv) ★★★ /daʊn/
end (n) ★★★ /end/
flower (n) ★★★ /ˈflaʊə/
ghost (n) ★★ /gəʊst/
group (n) ★★★ /gruːp/
guide (n) ★★★ /gaɪd/
guy (n) ★★ /gaɪ/
helmet (n) ★ /ˈhelmɪt/
including (prep) ★★★ /ɪnˈkluːdɪŋ/
jewellery (n) ★★ /ˈdʒuːəlri/
king (n) ★★★ /kɪŋ/
lady (n) ★★★ /ˈleɪdi/
line (n) ★★★ /laɪn/
magazine (n) ★★★ /ˌmægəˈziːn/
model (boat) (n) ★★★ /ˈmɒd(ə)l/
object (n) ★★★ /ˈɒbdʒekt/
out of (prep) /ˈaʊt ˌɒv/
part (= section) (n) ★★★ /pɑːt/

poster (n) ★★ /'pəʊstə/
ride (n) ★★ /raɪd/
sign (n) ★★★ /saɪn/
shark (n) ★ /ʃɑːk/
sightseeing (n) /'saɪtˌsiːɪŋ/
tomb (n) ★ /tuːm/
too (= as well) ★★★ /tuː/
tourist (n) ★★ /'tʊərɪst/
treasure (n) ★★ /'treʒə/
trumpet (n) ★ /'trʌmpɪt/
tunnel (n) ★★ /'tʌn(ə)l/
up (adv, prep) ★★★ /ʌp/
walk (n) ★★★ /wɔːk/
water sports (n pl) /'wɔːtə ˌspɔːts/
way (this way) (n) /weɪ/
★★★
woman (pl women) /'wʊmən/
(n) ★★★

ADJECTIVES

amazing (adj) ★★ /ə'meɪzɪŋ/
boring (adj) ★★ /'bɔːrɪŋ/
curly (hair) (adj) ★ /'kɜːli/
exciting (adj) ★★ /ɪk'saɪtɪŋ/
full of (adj) ★★★ /fʊl əv/
gold (adj) ★ /ɡəʊld/
hungry (adj) ★★ /'hʌŋɡri/
narrow (adj) ★★★ /'nærəʊ/
open-air (adj) /ˌəʊpən 'eə/
scared (adj) ★★ /skeəd/
scary (adj) ★ /'skeəri/
silver (adj) ★★ /'sɪlvə/
wonderful (adj) ★★★ /'wʌndəf(ə)l/

FURNITURE AND EQUIPMENT

blind (n) /blaɪnd/
board (n) ★★★ /bɔːd/
CD player (n) /siːdiː pleɪə/
chair (n) ★★★ /tʃeə/
chest of drawers (n) /ˌtʃest əv 'drɔːz/
computer (n) ★★★ /kəm'pjuːtə/
curtains (n pl) ★★ /'kɜːtənz/
desk (n) ★★★ /desk/
light(s) (n) ★★★ /laɪt/
table (n) ★★★ /'teɪb(ə)l/
wardrobe (n) ★ /'wɔːdrəʊb/

PARTS OF THE BODY

arm (n) ★★★ /ɑːm/
ear (n) ★★★ /ɪə/
eye (n) ★★★ /aɪ/
face (n) ★★★ /feɪs/
finger (n) ★★★ /'fɪŋɡə/
foot (pl feet) (n) ★★★ /fʊt/
hair (n) ★★★ /heə/
hand (n) ★★★ /hænd/
head (n) ★★★ /hed/
knee (n) ★★★ /niː/
leg (n) ★★★ /leɡ/
mouth (n) ★★★ /maʊθ/
nose (n) ★★★ /nəʊz/
thumb (n) ★★ /θʌm/
toe (n) ★★ /təʊ/
tooth (pl teeth) (n) /tuːθ/
★★★

TOWN FACILITIES AND ATTRACTIONS

aquarium (n) /ə'kweəriəm/
art gallery (n) /'ɑːt ˌɡæləri/
attraction (n) ★★ /ə'trækʃ(ə)n/
café (n) ★★ /'kæfeɪ/
funfair (n) /'fʌnˌfeə/
museum (n) ★★★ /mjuː'ziːəm/
pier (n) ★ /pɪə/
restaurant (n) ★★★ /'rest(ə)rɒnt/
shop (n) ★★★ /ʃɒp/
theatre (n) ★★★ /'θɪətə/

VERBS

hold (v) ★★★ /həʊld/
point (v) ★★★ /pɔɪnt/
rain (v) ★★ /reɪn/
rollerblade (v) /'rəʊləbleɪd/
sell (v) ★★★ /sel/
skateboard (v) /'skeɪtˌbɔːd/

smell (v) ★★ /smel/
stand (v) ★★★ /stænd/
wait (v) ★★★ /weɪt/
wash (v) ★★★ /wɒʃ/
wear (v) ★★★ /weə/
weigh (v) ★★ /weɪ/

EXPRESSIONS

clean your teeth /ˌkliːn jə 'tiːθ/
find out /ˌfaɪnd 'aʊt/
There isn't time. /ˌðeər ɪznt 'taɪm/
wash your hands /ˌwɒʃ jə 'hændz/

UNIT 5

ago (prep) ★★★ /ə'ɡəʊ/
alone (adv) ★★★ /ə'ləʊn/
around (prep) ★★★ /ə'raʊnd/
at the moment /ˌæt ðə 'məʊmənt/
cause (n) ★★★ /kɔːz/
centimetre (cm) (n) /'sentɪˌmiːtə/
coal (n) ★★★ /kəʊl/
coffee (n) ★★★ /'kɒfi/
conference (n) ★★★ /'kɒnf(ə)rəns/
crisps (n pl) ★ /krɪsps/
dolphin (n) ★ /'dɒlfɪn/
earring (n) ★ /'ɪərɪŋ/
energy (n) ★★★ /'enədʒi/
games console (n) /'ɡeɪmz ˌkɒnsəʊl/
gesture (n) ★★ /'dʒestʃə/
hospital (n) ★★★ /'hɒspɪt(ə)l/
idea (n) ★★★ /aɪ'dɪə/
island (n) ★★★ /'aɪlənd/
meaning (n) ★★★ /'miːnɪŋ/
midday (n) ★ /ˌmɪd'deɪ/
middle (n) ★★★ /'mɪd(ə)l/
news (n) ★★★ /njuːz/
next (adv) ★★★ /nekst/
noon (n) ★ /nuːn/
nothing (pron) ★★★ /'nʌθɪŋ/
oil (n) ★★★ /ɔɪl/
outside (adv) ★★★ /ˌaʊt'saɪd/
personality test (n) /pɜːsə'næləti ˌtest/
plane (n) ★★★ /pleɪn/
planet (n) ★★ /'plænɪt/
quickly (adv) ★★★ /'kwɪkli/
quiz (n) ★ /kwɪz/
radio (n) ★★★ /'reɪdiəʊ/
remote (n) /rɪ'məʊt/
sea level (n) /'siː ˌlevl/
score (n) ★★★ /skɔː/
star (in the sky) (n) /stɑː/
★★★
tea (n) ★★★ /tiː/
toast (n) ★ /təʊst/

ADJECTIVES

bad (adj) ★★★ /bæd/
central (adj) ★★★ /'sentrəl/
crazy (adj) ★★ /'kreɪzi/
difficult (adj) ★★★ /'dɪfɪk(ə)lt/
fabulous (adj) ★ /'fæbjʊləs/
funny (adj) ★★★ /'fʌni/
high (adj) ★★★ /haɪ/
hurt (adj) /hɜːt/
ill (adj) ★★★ /ɪl/
important (adj) ★★★ /ɪm'pɔːt(ə)nt/
man-made (adj) /ˌmæn'meɪd/
northern (adj) ★★★ /'nɔːðən/
typical (adj) ★★★ /'tɪpɪk(ə)l/

JOBS

cleaner (n) ★ /'kliːnə/
doctor (n) ★★★ /'dɒktə/
electrician (n) /ɪˌlek'trɪʃ(ə)n/
fire-fighter (n) /'faɪəˌfaɪtə/
hairdresser (n) ★ /'heəˌdresə/
interpreter (n) ★ /ɪn'tɜːprɪtə/
journalist (n) ★★ /'dʒɜːnəlɪst/
model (n & v) ★★★ /'mɒd(ə)l/
musician (n) ★★ /mjuː'zɪʃ(ə)n/
nurse (n) ★★★ /nɜːs/
pilot (n) ★★ /'paɪlət/
police (n pl) ★★★ /pə'liːs/
police officer (n) ★ /pə'liːs ˌɒfɪsə/
scientist (n) ★★★ /'saɪəntɪst/

shop assistant (n) /'ʃɒp əˌsɪstənt/
taxi-driver (n) /'tæksiˌdraɪvə/
teacher (n) ★★★ /'tiːtʃə/
waiter (n) ★ /'weɪtə/

PERSONALITY AND FEELINGS

careful (adj) ★★★ /'keəf(ə)l/
confident (adj) ★★ /'kɒnfɪd(ə)nt/
cross (adj) /krɒs/
friendly (adj) ★★★ /'fren(d)li/
happy (adj) ★★★ /'hæpi/
helpful (adj) ★★ /'helpf(ə)l/
open (adj) ★★★ /'əʊpən/
quiet (adj) ★★★ /'kwaɪət/
serious (adj) ★★★ /'sɪəriəs/
shy (adj) ★ /ʃaɪ/

PUNCTUATION

brackets (n) ★ /'brækɪts/
capital letter (n) /ˌkæpɪtl 'letə/
comma (n) ★ /'kɒmə/
exclamation mark (n) /eksklə'meɪʃn ˌmɑːk/
full stop (n) ★ /ˌfʊl stɒp/
hyphen (n) /'haɪf(ə)n/
question mark (n) ★ /'kwestʃən ˌmɑːk/

VERBS

change (n & v) ★★★ /tʃeɪndʒ/
compare (v) ★★★ /kəm'peə/
discuss (v) ★★★ /dɪ'skʌs/
expand (v) ★★★ /ɪk'spænd/
feel (v) ★★★ /fiːl/
fly (v) ★★★ /flaɪ/
fold (your arms) (v) ★★ /fəʊld/
get (= become) (v) ★★★ /ɡet/
happen (v) ★★★ /'hæpən/
laugh (v) ★★★ /lɑːf/
look after (v) /ˌlʊk 'ɑːftə/
look for (v) /'lʊk ˌfɔː, fə/
melt (v) ★★ /melt/
sail (v) ★★ /seɪl/
shop (v) ★★ /ʃɒp/
shout (v) ★★★ /ʃaʊt/
smile (v) ★★★ /smaɪl/
sneeze (v) /sniːz/
sunbathe (v) /'sʌnˌbeɪð/
touch (v) ★★★ /tʌtʃ/
translate (v) ★★ /træns'leɪt/
vary (v) ★★★ /'veəri/

WEATHER AND CLIMATE

autumn (n) ★★★ /'ɔːtəm/
climate change (n) /'klaɪmət ˌtʃeɪndʒ/
cloudy (adj) /'klaʊdi/
cold (adj) ★★★ /kəʊld/
degree (n) ★★★ /dɪ'ɡriː/
dry (adj) ★★★ /draɪ/
foggy (adj) /'fɒɡi/
hot (adj) ★★★ /hɒt/
ice (n) ★★★ /aɪs/
rain (n & v) ★★★ /reɪn/
rainy (adj) /'reɪni/
shine (v) ★★ /ʃaɪn/
snow (n & v) ★★★ /snəʊ/
snowy (adj) /'snəʊi/
spring (n) ★★★ /sprɪŋ/
sun (n) ★★★ /sʌn/
sunny (adj) ★ /'sʌni/
temperature (n) ★★★ /'temprɪtʃə/
tropics (n pl) /'trɒpɪks/
warm (adj) ★★★ /wɔːm/
weather (n) ★★★ /'weðə/
wet (adj) ★★★ /wet/
windy (adj) ★ /'wɪndi/

EXPRESSIONS

Bless you! /'bles ˌjuː/
for example /ˌfər ɪɡ'zɑːmpl/
go to sleep /ˌɡəʊ tə 'sliːp/
Goodbye. ★ /ˌɡʊd'baɪ/
Good idea. /ˌɡʊd aɪ'dɪə/
good luck /ˌɡʊd 'lʌk/
have a wonderful time /hæv ə ˌwʌndəfl 'taɪm/
have a word /ˌhæv ə 'wɜːd/
How do you do? /ˌhaʊ də ju 'duː/
Well done! /wel 'dʌn/
What do you do? /ˌwɒt də ju 'duː/

WORD LIST

UNIT 6

across (prep) ★★★	/ə'krɒs/
almost (adv) ★★★	/'ɔːlməʊst/
archaeologist (n) ★	/ɑːki'ɒlədʒɪst/
artist (n) ★★★	/'ɑːtɪst/
at first (adv)	/ˌət 'fɜːst/
beer (n) ★★★	/bɪə/
blood (n) ★★★	/blʌd/
board game (n)	/'bɔːd ˌgeɪm/
bread (n) ★★★	/bred/
by (train) (prep)	/baɪ/
castle (n) ★★	/'kɑːs(ə)l/
champion (n) ★★★	/'tʃæmpiən/
clue (n) ★★	/kluː/
dice game (n)	/'daɪs ˌgeɪm/
dog (n) ★★★	/dɒg/
dress (n) ★★★	/dres/
DVD (n) ★★	/ˌdiː viː 'diː/
explorer (n)	/ɪk'splɔːrə/
finally (adv) ★★★	/'faɪn(ə)li/
forward (adv) ★★	/'fɔːwəd/
host (n) ★★	/həʊst/
land (n) ★★★	/lænd/
meanwhile (adv) ★★★	/'miːnˌwaɪl/
minibus (n)	/'mɪniˌbʌs/
moon (n) ★★	/muːn/
no one (pron) ★★★	/nəʊ wʌn/
park (n) ★★★	/pɑːk/
pirate (n)	/'paɪrət/
president (n) ★★★	/'prezɪdənt/
prince (n) ★★	/prɪns/
ship (n) ★★★	/ʃɪp/
shopping centre (n)	/'ʃɒpɪŋ ˌsentə/
silver (n) ★★	/'sɪlvə/
step (n) ★★★	/step/
storm (n) ★★	/stɔːm/
story (n) ★★★	/'stɔːri/
straight (adv) ★★★	/streɪt/
through (prep) ★★★	/θruː/
together (adv) ★★★	/tə'geðə/
train (n) ★★★	/treɪn/
vampire (n)	/'væmpaɪə/
vegetable (n) ★★★	/'vedʒtəb(ə)l/
volcano (n) ★	/vɒl'keɪnəʊ/
yesterday (adv) ★★★	/'jestədeɪ/

ADJECTIVES

dead (adj) ★★★	/ded/
fair (hair) (adj) ★★★	/feə/
false (adj) ★★	/fɔːls/
huge (adj) ★★★	/hjuːdʒ/
last (night) (adj) ★★★	/lɑːst/
only (adj) ★★★	/'əʊnli/
primary (adj) ★★★	/'praɪməri/
real (adj) ★★★	/rɪəl/
strange (adj) ★★★	/streɪndʒ/
strong (adj) ★★★	/strɒŋ/
tall (adj) ★★★	/tɔːl/
terrible (adj) ★★★	/'terəb(ə)l/
true (adj) ★★★	/truː/

CONTINENTS

Africa	/'æfrɪkə/
Asia	/'eɪʒə/
Europe	/'jʊərəp/
North America	/ˌnɔːθ ə'merɪkə/
South America	/ˌsaʊθ ə'merɪkə/

FEELINGS

angry (adj) ★★★	/'æŋgri/
cross (adj)	/krɒs/
happy (adj) ★★★	/'hæpi/
sad (adj) ★★★	/sæd/
scared (adj) ★★	/skeəd/
surprised (adj) ★★★	/sə'praɪzd/
worried (adj) ★★★	/'wʌrid/

VERBS

agree (v) ★★★	/ə'griː/
attack (v) ★★★	/ə'tæk/
become (v) ★★★	/bɪ'kʌm/
call (= phone) (v) ★★★	/kɔːl/
carry (v) ★★★	/'kæri/
come from (v)	/kʌm ˌfrɒm/
crash (v) ★★	/kræʃ/
cycle (v) ★	/'saɪk(ə)l/

decide (v) ★★★	/dɪ'saɪd/
die (v) ★★★	/daɪ/
drink (v) ★★★	/drɪŋk/
escape (v) ★★★	/ɪ'skeɪp/
go back (v)	/ˌgəʊ 'bæk/
jump (v) ★★★	/dʒʌmp/
kill (v) ★★★	/kɪl/
kiss (v) ★★★	/kɪs/
look (worried) (v) ★★★	/lʊk/
lose (v) ★★★	/luːz/
return (v) ★★★	/rɪ'tɜːn/
save (v) ★★★	/seɪv/
steal (v) ★★★	/stiːl/
turn (v) ★★★	/tɜːn/
win (v) ★★★	/wɪn/

EXPRESSIONS

all right ★★★	/ˌɔːl 'raɪt/
on my own	/ˌɒn maɪ 'əʊn/
to be honest	/ˌtu biː 'ɒnɪst/
What's the matter?	/ˌwɒts ðə 'mætə/

UNIT 7

adult (n) ★★★	/'ædʌlt, ə'dʌlt/
as well as	/əz 'wel æz/
aunt (n) ★★★	/ɑːnt/
back (at the back) (n) ★★★	/bæk/
barbecue (n) ★	/'bɑːbɪˌkjuː/
because (conj) ★★★	/bɪ'kɒz/
championship (n) ★★★	/'tʃæmpiənʃɪp/
competition (n) ★★★	/ˌkɒmpə'tɪʃ(ə)n/
cowboy (n)	/'kaʊˌbɔɪ/
flight (n) ★★★	/flaɪt/
housework (n) ★★	/'haʊsˌwɜːk/
lifestyle (n) ★★	/'laɪfˌstaɪl/
marriage (n) ★★★	/'mærɪdʒ/
most (adv) ★★★	/məʊst/
mostly (adv) ★★★	/'məʊs(t)li/
pet (n) ★★	/pet/
plan (n) ★★★	/plæn/
player (n) ★★★	/pleɪə/
prize (n) ★★★	/praɪz/
programme (= TV) (n) ★★★	/'prəʊgræm/
ranch (n)	/rɑːntʃ/
slowly (adv) ★★★	/'sləʊli/
speed (n) ★★★	/spiːd/
uncle (n) ★★	/'ʌŋk(ə)l/
university (n) ★★★	/ˌjuːnɪ'vɜːsəti/
way (n) ★★★	/weɪ/
winner (n) ★★★	/'wɪnə/

ADJECTIVES

correct (adj) ★★★	/kə'rekt/
dangerous (adj) ★★★	/'deɪndʒərəs/
excellent (adj) ★★★	/'eksələnt/
fast (adj) ★★★	/fɑːst/
large (adj) ★★★	/lɑːdʒ/
level (adj) ★★	/'lev(ə)l/
slow (adj) ★★★	/sləʊ/
ugly (adj) ★★	/'ʌgli/
unhappy (adj) ★★	/ʌn'hæpi/
weekly (adj) ★★	/'wiːkli/
young (adj) ★★★	/jʌŋ/

ANIMALS

animal (n) ★★★	/'ænɪm(ə)l/
bird (n) ★★★	/bɜːd/
camel (n)	/'kæm(ə)l/
cat (n) ★★★	/kæt/
cheetah (n)	/'tʃiːtə/
cobra (n)	/'kəʊbrə/
cow (n) ★★	/kaʊ/
dog (n) ★★★	/dɒg/
elephant (n) ★	/'elɪfənt/
falcon (n)	/'fɔːlkən/
giraffe (n) ★	/dʒə'rɑːf/
hippo (n)	/'hɪpəʊ/
horse (n) ★★★	/hɔːs/
insect (n) ★★	/'ɪnsekt/
kangaroo (n)	/ˌkæŋgə'ruː/
lion (n) ★★	/'laɪən/
monkey (n) ★	/'mʌŋki/
mosquito (n)	/mɒ'skiːtəʊ/

octopus (n)	/'ɒktəpəs/
parrot (n) ★	/'pærət/
penguin (n)	/'peŋgwɪn/
polar bear (n)	/'pəʊlə ˌbeə/
rabbit (n) ★★	/'ræbɪt/
sailfish (n)	/'seɪlˌfɪʃ/
shark (n) ★	/ʃɑːk/
sheep (n) ★★★	/ʃiːp/
snake (n) ★	/sneɪk/
tiger (n) ★	/'taɪgə/
whale (n) ★★	/weɪl/

FOOD AND DRINK

fast food (n) ★	/ˌfɑːst 'fuːd/
frozen food (n)	/ˌfrəʊzn 'fuːd/
grain (n) ★★	/greɪn/
milk (n) ★★★	/mɪlk/
porridge (n)	/'pɒrɪdʒ/
rice (n) ★★	/raɪs/
stew (n)	/stjuː/

HEALTH AND ILLNESS

accident (n) ★★★	/'æksɪd(ə)nt/
ambulance (n) ★★	/'æmbjʊləns/
bite (n) ★	/baɪt/
disease (n) ★★★	/dɪ'ziːz/
healthy (adj) ★★★	/'helθi/
hospital (n) ★★★	/'hɒspɪt(ə)l/
hurt (v) (v) ★★★	/hɜːt/
ill (adj) ★★★	/ɪl/
malaria (n)	/mə'leəriə/
medicine (n) ★★	/'med(ə)s(ə)n/
X-ray (n & v) ★	/'eksˌreɪ/

LEISURE ACTIVITIES

chess (n) ★	/tʃes/
dancing (n) ★	/'dɑːnsɪŋ/
drawing (n) ★★★	/'drɔːɪŋ/
fishing (n) ★★	/'fɪʃɪŋ/
ice hockey (n)	/'aɪs ˌhɒki/
knitting (n) ★	/'nɪtɪŋ/
painting (n) ★★★	/'peɪntɪŋ/
riding (n)	/'raɪdɪŋ/
rollerblading (n)	/'rəʊləˌbleɪdɪŋ/
sailing (n)	/'seɪlɪŋ/
skateboarding (n)	/'skeɪtˌbɔːdɪŋ/
skydiving (n)	/'skaɪˌdaɪvɪŋ/
snowboarding (n)	/'snəʊˌbɔːdɪŋ/
surfing (n)	/'sɜːfɪŋ/
swimming (n) ★	/'swɪmɪŋ/

VERBS

dive (v) ★★	/daɪv/
finish (v) ★★★	/'fɪnɪʃ/
go out (v)	/ˌgəʊ 'aʊt/
include (v) ★★★	/ɪn'kluːd/
knit (v) ★	/nɪt/
prepare (v) ★★★	/prɪ'peə/
ring back (v)	/ˌrɪŋ 'bæk/
share (v) ★★★	/ʃeə/
suggest (v) ★★★	/sə'dʒest/
surf (n & v) ★	/sɜːf/
travel (n & v) ★★★	/'træv(ə)l/
turn on (a computer) (v)	/ˌtɜːn 'ɒn/

EXPRESSIONS

have fun	/ˌhæv 'fʌn/
lose weight	/ˌluːz 'weɪt/
spend time	/ˌspend 'taɪm/
take medicine	/ˌteɪk 'medsn/

UNIT 8

allowance (n) ★★	/ə'laʊəns/
amount (n) ★★★	/ə'maʊnt/
anyone (pron) ★★★	/'eniˌwʌn/
arrival (n) ★★★	/ə'raɪv(ə)l/
bank account (n) ★	/'bæŋk əˌkaʊnt/
beginning (n) ★★★	/bɪ'gɪnɪŋ/
buffet (n)	/'bʊfeɪ/
camera phone (n)	/'kæmrə ˌfəʊn/
club (n) ★★★	/klʌb/
cooking (n) ★★	/'kʊkɪŋ/
culture (n) ★★★	/'kʌltʃə/
during (prep) ★★★	/'djʊərɪŋ/
go ice-skating	/ˌgəʊ 'aɪs ˌskeɪtɪŋ/

hobby (n) ★	/ˈhɒbi/
invitation (n) ★★	/ˌɪnvɪˈteɪʃ(ə)n/
journey (n) ★★★	/ˈdʒɜːni/
loads (of) (n pl) ★★	/ˈləʊdz (əv)/
nationality (n) ★	/ˌnæʃəˈnæləti/
normally (adv) ★★★	/ˈnɔːm(ə)li/
paradise (n) ★	/ˈpærədaɪs/
pocket money (n) ★	/ˈpɒkɪt ˌmʌni/
pound (£) (n) ★★★	/ˈpaʊnd/
rhythm (n) ★★	/ˈrɪðəm/
skateboard (n)	/ˈskeɪtˌbɔːd/
suggestion (n) ★★★	/səˈdʒestʃ(ə)n/
thank-you letter (n)	/ˈθæŋkjuː ˌletə/

ADJECTIVES

connected (with) (adj) ★	/kəˈnektɪd (wɪð,wɪθ)/
delicious (adj) ★	/dɪˈlɪʃəs/
excited (adj) ★★	/ɪkˈsaɪtɪd/
filled (adj)	/fɪld/
kind (adj) ★	/kaɪnd/
little (adj) ★★★	/ˈlɪt(ə)l/
normal (adj) ★★★	/ˈnɔːm(ə)l/
paper (adj)	/ˈpeɪpə/
plastic (adj) ★★★	/ˈplæstɪk/
recent (adj) ★★★	/ˈriːs(ə)nt/
rich (adj) ★★★	/rɪtʃ/
safe (adj) ★★★	/seɪf/
thirsty (adj) ★	/ˈθɜːsti/
vegetarian (adj)	/ˌvedʒəˈteəriən/

FOOD AND DRINK

apple (n) ★★	/ˈæp(ə)l/
apple juice (n) ★	/ˈæp(ə)l dʒuːs/
chocolate cake (n)	/tʃɒklət keɪk/
fruit juice (n)	/ˈfruːt ˌdʒuːs/
fruit salad (n)	/ˌfruːt ˈsæləd/
hamburger (n)	/ˈhæmˌbɜːgə/
kebab (n)	/kɪˈbæb/
orange (n) ★★	/ˈɒrɪndʒ/
sandwich (n) ★★	/ˈsæn(d)wɪdʒ, ˈsæn(d)wɪtʃ/
sausage (n) ★	/ˈsɒsɪdʒ/
tomato salad (n)	/təˌmɑːtəʊ ˈsæləd/

KITCHEN

cooker (n) ★	/ˈkʊkə/
cup (n) ★★★	/kʌp/
dishwasher (n)	/ˈdɪʃˌwɒʃə/
fork (n) ★	/fɔːk/
fridge (n) ★	/frɪdʒ/
glass (n) ★★★	/glɑːs/
knife (pl knives) (n) ★★★	/naɪf/
plate (n) ★★★	/pleɪt/
spoon (n) ★	/spuːn/
washing machine (n) ★	/ˈwɒʃɪŋ məˌʃiːn/

VERBS

accept (v) ★★★	/əkˈsept/
arrive (v) ★★★	/əˈraɪv/
bring (v) ★★★	/brɪŋ/
celebrate (v) ★★★	/ˈseləˌbreɪt/
cost (v) ★★★	/kɒst/
drop (v) ★★★	/drɒp/
invite (v) ★★★	/ɪnˈvaɪt/
mind (v) ★★★	/maɪnd/
miss (v) ★★★	/mɪs/
offer (v) ★★★	/ˈɒfə/
show (v) ★★★	/ʃəʊ/
thank (v) ★★★	/θæŋk/

EXPRESSIONS

all sorts (of)	/ˈɔːl ˌsɔːts (əv)/
get on (well)	/ˈget ˌɒn (wel)/
hang around	/ˌhæŋ əˈraʊnd/
hard work	/ˌhɑːd ˈwɜːk/
I'd love to.	/aɪd ˈlʌv tuː/
Let me know.	/ˌlet miː ˈnəʊ/
look forward to	/ˌlʊk ˈfɔːwəd tuː/
make an excuse	/ˌmeɪk ən ɪkˈskjuːs/
Many thanks (for …)	/ˌmeni ˈθæŋks (fɔː)/
on average	/ˌɒn ˈævrɪdʒ/
spend money (on)	/ˌspend ˈmʌni (ɒn)/

PRONUNCIATION GUIDE

Vowels

/ɑː/	arm, large
/æ/	cap, bad
/aɪ/	ride, fly
/aɪə/	diary, science
/aʊ/	how, mouth
/aʊə/	our, shower
/e/	bed, head
/eɪ/	day, grey
/eə/	hair, there
/ɪ/	give, did
/i/	happy, taxi
/iː/	we, heat
/ɪə/	ear, here
/ɒ/	not, watch
/əʊ/	cold, boat
/ɔː/	door, talk
/ɔɪ/	point, boy
/ʊ/	foot, could
/uː/	two, food
/ʊə/	sure, tourist
/ɜː/	bird, heard
/ʌ/	fun, come
/ə/	mother, actor

Consonants

/b/	bag, rubbish
/d/	desk, cold
/f/	fill, laugh
/g/	girl, big
/h/	hand, home
/j/	yes, young
/k/	cook, back
/l/	like, fill
/m/	mean, climb
/n/	new, want
/p/	park, happy
/r/	ring, borrow
/s/	say, this
/t/	town, city
/v/	very, live
/w/	water, away
/z/	zoo, his
/ʃ/	shop, machine
/ʒ/	usually, television
/ŋ/	thank, doing
/tʃ/	cheese, picture
/θ/	thing, north
/ð/	that, clothes
/dʒ/	jeans, bridge

IRREGULAR VERBS

Infinitive	Past simple
be	was, were
become	became
begin	began
bite	bit
bring	brought
burn	burnt/burned
buy	bought
catch	caught
choose	chose
come	came
cost	cost
cut	cut
do	did
draw	drew
drink	drank
drive	drove
eat	ate
fall	fell
feel	felt
find	found
fly	flew
forget	forgot
get	got
give	gave
go	went
hang	hung
have	had
hear	heard
hide	hid
hold	held
hurt	hurt
keep	kept
know	knew
learn	learnt/learned
leave	left
lend	lent
let	let
lose	lost
make	made
mean	meant
meet	met
pay	paid
put	put
read /riːd/	read /red/
ride	rode
ring	rang
run	ran
say	said
see	saw
sell	sold
send	sent
sew	sewed
shine	shone
show	showed
sing	sang
sit	sat
sleep	slept
smell	smelt/smelled
speak	spoke
spell	spelt/spelled
spend	spent
stand	stood
steal	stole
swim	swam
take	took
teach	taught
tell	told
think	thought
understand	understood
wear	wore
win	won
write	wrote

Macmillan Education
4 Crinan Street
London N1 9XW
A division of Springer Nature Limited
Companies and representatives throughout the world

ISBN 978-0-230-40847-0

Text © Judy Garton-Sprenger and Philip Prowse 2011
Design and illustration © Springer Nature Limited 2011

First published 2011

Original design by Giles Davies
Page make-up by eMC Design Ltd
Illustrated by Arlene Adams pp11(m), 25; Jamel Akib pp82, 83, 85; Adrian Barclay
pp11(t), 15, 21, 113; Kathy Baxendale pp37, 46(l); Paul Cemmick p98(b); Giles Davies
pp13, 43, 45, 114; Mark Duffin p57; ODI pp22-23, 48, 49; Ruth Palmer pp36, 39, 47,
62, 103, 111; Martin Sanders pp55, 63, 78-79; Kate Sheppard pp20, 46(r), 72, 98(t);
Mike Spoor p53; Victor Tavares pp70-71; Laszlo Veres pp95(t), 99; Nadine Wickenden
pp95(b), 105.
Cover design by Designers Collective
Cover photos by **Alamy**/ Mark Beton/ England (tl), Alamy/ Robert Harding Picture
Library (bcl), **Corbis**/ Moodboard (tcl), **Getty**/ (bl), Getty/ Oliver Benn (tcr), Getty/
Peter Cade (bcr), **Jupiter**/ Brand X Pictures (br), **Photolibrary**/ Eric Sanford (tr).

The authors would like to thank all the team at Macmillan Education in the UK and
worldwide for everything they have done to create *New Inspiration*. We are most
grateful to Celia Bingham for editing the Student's Book, to Helena Gomm for revising
the Workbook, and to Rachel Bladon and Anna Cole for the Teacher's Book. We would
also like to thank James Richardson for his usual great skill in producing the recorded
material, and the actors who appear on the recordings and bring the book to life.

We owe an enormous debt of gratitude to teenage students and their teachers in many
different countries who welcomed us into their classrooms and contributed so much
to the formation of *New Inspiration*. In particular we would like to thank teachers and
classes in Argentina, Greece, Italy, Poland, Spain, Switzerland, Turkey and Uruguay.
We are equally indebted to all those participants on teacher training courses in Europe,
South America and elsewhere from whom we have learnt so much, in particular British
Council courses in the UK and overseas, and courses at the University of Durham and
NILE in Norwich.

The authors and publishers would like to express their great thanks to all those who
commented on syllabus and materials for *New Inspiration* and provided feedback
on their use of *Inspiration*, in particular: Fatiha Ajaoui, Mª Angeles Ramiro Alvarez,
Alejandro De Angelis, Asun Armendáriz, Roseli Franco Babora, Cristina Ceratti Bo,
Monika Bucher, Barbara Chuck, Bilsev Demir, Anastasia Egorova, Yolanda Elsener-
Fischer, Pia Ettlin, Nadine Fesseler, Katharina Fischer, Joe Hediger, Lisbeth Heinzer-
Föhn, Alda Heloisa Santoyo Garcia, Anna Häfliger-Schmidlin, Mgr.Jana Hanesova,
Katharina Hofmann, Corinna Iaizzo, Daniela Iskerková, Estrella Gómez Jiménez-
Tusset, Bulent Karababa, Figen Kılıçarslan, Antonia Köppel, Svetlana Korostelyova,
Lycia Lourenço Lacerda, Carmelia Loher, Pilar García López-Tello, Zuzana Lovasova,
Monika Mižáková, Fabiane R. Montanari, Andrea Cristina Neiger, Clara González
O'Sullivan, Ingrid Rizzi Razente, Brigitte Reber, Peach Richmond, Alfonsa Pliego
Romera, Jean Rüdiger-Harper, Karl Russi, Monica Cristina Sales, Susanna Schwab,
Adilson Geraldo Da Silva, Monica Dolores Sosa, Geraldo de Souza Jr, Janine Strub-
Dittli, Maria Vertiletskaya, Mª Rosa Pradilla Vicente, Maria Luisa Villarruel, Menekşe
Yildiz, Andrea Zeiger.

The authors and publishers would like to thank the following for permission to
reproduce their photographic material:
Alamy/ Valerie Armstrong p40(l), Alamy/ Joanne Baines p13(bike), Alamy/ Mark
Beton p14(background), Alamy/ Tom Brakefield p94(tr), Alamy/ Franck Camhi
p63(c), Alamy/ John Cooper p20(supermarket), Alamy/ CoverSpot p20(taxi), Alamy/
Simon Cowling p20(bar), Alamy/ Ian Dagnall p77(tr), Alamy/ Kate Diamond p77(br),
Alamy/ Mark Dyball p20(tourist info), Alamy/ Chad Ehlers p65(tl), Alamy/ Roger
Eritja p94(tl), Alamy/ Kevin Foy p62(tl), 77(cr), Alamy/ Stephen Frink Collection
p94(cr), Alamy/ John Fryer p58(tr), Alamy/ Horizon International Images Limited
p15(tl), Alamy/ Chris Howes/ Wild Places Photography p54(tl), Alamy/ Images of

Africa Photobank pp89(ctl), 96(cb), Alamy/ Image Source p94(bl), Alamy/ James
Ingle p81(background), Alamy/ INSADCO Photography p74(cr), Alamy/ Tim Jones
p80(background), Alamy/ Juniors Bildarchiv p31(tl), Alamy/ Jason Lindsey p96(b),
Alamy/ Mar Photographics p69(br), Alamy/ Dean Mitchell p74(bl), Alamy/ Mitchel's
Photography p69(tr), Alamy/ David L Moore p58(tl), Alamy/ nagelestock.com p69(cr),
Alamy/ NetPhotos p27(tcr), Alamy/ Nick Lewis Photography p27(tl), Alamy/ Dave
Porter p50(br), Alamy/ Jose Manuel Revuelta Luna p20(restaurant), Alamy/ Robert
Harding Picture Library Ltd p50-51(background), Alamy/ RubberBall p74(cl),
Alamy/ Alistair Scott p20(police), Alamy/ Alex Segre p77(bl), Alamy/ Edward Simons
p52(background), Alamy/ Stock Italia p20(hotel), Alamy/ Jocken Tack p18(t), Alamy/
Tetra Images p75, Alamy/ Vontica p27(br), Alamy/ David K Werk p24(bl), 59(bl),
Alamy/ Wherrett.com p94(br), Alamy/ Richard Williams pp8-9(background), Alamy/
Chris Young p20(camping); **BBC Motion Gallery**/ pp36(b), 40(r); **Brand X**/ p89(3);
Corbis/ pp21(tr), 89(1), Corbis/ Rolf Bruderer p27(tc), Corbis/ John Bryson/Sygma
p76(tcr), Corbis/ Sean Davey/Australian Picture Library p96(c), Corbis/ Kevin Dodge
p48(t), Corbis/ Randy Faris p27(cct), Corbis/ Peter M. Fisher pp28, 63(cl), 65(cr), 73(tr),
Corbis/ Armando Gallo/Retna Ltd p8(cr), Corbis/ Kristy-Anne Glubish/Design Pics
p97, Corbis/ Image Source pp11(tr), 24(bcr), Corbis/ Susanne Kronholm/Etsa p110(b),
Corbis/ Beau Lark p58(br), Corbis/ Scott Legato/ Retna Ltd pp30-31(t), 33(bl), Corbis/
Danny Lehman p63(t), Corbis/ Theowulf Maehl p69(cl), Corbis/ Robert Michael
p86(tl), Corbis/ Moodboard p34, Corbis/ David A. Northcott p94(2), Corbis/ Ocean
pp10(c), 16, 21, 65(tr), Corbis/ Jose Luis Pelaez, Inc./Blend Images p74(tl), Corbis/
Denis Scott p94(4), Corbis/ Onne van der Wal p64, 73(tl), Corbis/ Mirek Weichsel/
First Light p50(r inset), Corbis/ Allana Wesley White pp37(tr), 49(l), Corbis/ Liu
Yongqiu/Xinhua Press pp68-69(b); **Creatas**/ p89(4); **Digital Stock**/ pp15(tr, bl), 69(bl);
Kenneth Garrett/ pp37(tl), 56; **Getty**/ pp8(bl), 13(14), 17(ct), 20(photo), 27(bl), 33(cr),
84(r), 89(tr), 92(bl, t), 93(b), Getty/ Oliver Benn p18(c), Getty/ Judy Bishop - The
Travelling Eye p110(t), Getty/ Bloomberg p63(b), Getty/ Peter Cade pp27(bc), 33(tl),
Getty/ Hola Images p24(bcl), Getty/ Image Source p24(tr), Getty/ Bob Langrish p105,
Getty/ Allison Michael Orenstein p65(cl), Getty/ Jose Luis Pelaez Inc p74(tr), Getty/
Charles P.Polk and Charles W.Peale p76(tr), Getty/ Stockbyte p54(tr), Getty/ Time &
Life Pictures p112, Getty/ WireImage p8(br); **Goodshoot**/ p63(cb); Guardian News
& Media Ltd 2009/ Felix Clay and David Mansell pp89(Emil & Freya), 104; **Image
Source**/ p63(ct); **Caroline Irby Photography**/ p106; **IT Stock Free RF**/ p74(br);
Macmillan Publishers Ltd/Dean Ryan pp11(3), 13(6), 21(b), Macmillan Publishers
Australia Ltd/ p27(bcr), Macmillan Publishers Ltd/ Haddon Davies p86(earrings,
1,2,3,4,5), Macmillan Publishers Ltd/ David Tolley p11(2), Macmillan Publishers Ltd/
David Tolley/ Rob Judges p86(br), Macmillan Publishers Ltd/ David Tolley/ Dean Ryan
p13(16); **Mary Evans Picture Library**/ p76(cl); **Medio Images**/ p69(tl); **Peter Menzel**/
www.menzelphoto.com p100; **Merlin Entertainments Group**/ p50(cb); **Nature
Picture Library**/ Mark Payne-Gill p94(br); **Photodisc**/ p89(2, 5); **Photolibrary**/
p38(background), Photolibrary/ Best View Stock p76(bcl), Photolibrary/ Bluemoon
Images p65(bl), Photolibrary/ ComStock p59(r), Photolibrary/ Cahir Davitt p20(cafe),
Photolibrary/ De Agostini Editore p76(bl), Photolibrary/ Nigel Dennis p94(cl),
Photolibrary/ Franck Dunouau p77(tl), Photolibrary/ Ingram Publishing p54(br),
Photolibrary/ Joff Lee p27(ccb), Photolibrary/ Keith Levit p96(ct), Photolibrary/
Mattes Mattes p15(br), Photolibrary/ Pacific Stock pp96(t), 99, Photolibrary/
PhotosIndia p27(tr), Photolibrary/ Eric Sanford p50(l inset), Photolibrary/ Superstock
Inc p48(b), Photolibrary/ Tips Italia RF p92(br), Photolibrary/ White p18(b);
Punchstock/ Design Pics p31(c & br); **Rex Features**/ pp30(b), 44, 47(b), Rex Features/
Anglia Press Agency Ltd p60, Rex Features/ Canadian Press p76(tl), Rex Features/ EPS
p17(cb), Rex Features/ Image Source p27(bcl), Rex Features/ Lehtikuva OY p17(tl), Rex
Features/ National Geographic/ Everett p84(l), Rex Features/ Gregory Pace/ BEI p17(bl),
Rex Features/ Startraks Photo pp17(r), 76(bcr), 93(inset); **Superstock**/ pp24(br), 49(b);
www.apple.com/ p13(2).

P82 Macmillan Reader Dracula cover image by Dracula from the Myths Series © Andy
Warhol/ Warhol Foundation/ Corbis.

Commissioned photography by:
Stuart Cox pp 8(t, m), 6,7,10(a, c), 12,14,18(portraits), 19, 26, 28, 33(girl), 36(t), 37(d,
e), 38, 39, 42, 45, 47(t), 52, 59(tl), 62(b, c), 65(br), 66, 67, 73(b), 80, 81, 85, 88, 89(c), 90,
102, 107, 111.
Paul Bricknell pp 11(1,4, 5, 6), 13(1, 3, 4, 5), 7,8, 9,10,11,12,13,15), 20(wallet, pen, comb,
camera, key, map, clock, ticket, calculator, umbrella, ID card), 21(a, c, d, e).

Cover credits:
Alamy/ Mark Beton/ England (tl), Alamy/ Robert Harding Picture Library (bcl),
Corbis/ Moodboard (tcl), **Getty**/ (bl) Getty/ Oliver Benn (tcr), Getty/ Peter Cade (bcr),
Jupiter/ Brand X Pictures (br), **Photolibrary**/ Eric Sanford (tr).

Dictionary extracts taken from Macmillan Essential Dictionary copyright © Macmillan
Publishers Limited 2003 and Macmillan English Dictionary 2nd Edition copyright ©
Macmillan Publishers Limited 2007

Printed and bound in Poland by CGS

2022 2021 2020 2019
26 25 24 23 22 21